Norbert Kilian

They come back

Rebirth and soul migration of our pets

BoD - Books on Demand, Norderstedt

ISBN 978-3-7526-4473-9

"The doctrine of reincarnation is neither absurd nor useless. Being reborn twice is not more astonishing than once.
Resurrection is natures key."
according to Voltaire, philosopher

DEAR READER!

I am very pleased that this book is now also available in English. My wife has translated it with the help of several programs. Some friends read and also corrected it. Nevertheless, it is grammatically and orthographically not perfect, but that is not bad, because the most important thing is the content.

The subtitle of this book is "Rebirth and soul migration of our pets". I am convinced that every living being has a soul and so every living being can either go to heaven or be reborn. Every animal can come back to us.

The fact that this book so often talks about dogs and cats is only because I have found very few reports about other reborn animals. A dog owner lives closely together with his dog, usually in his flat. This means that he sees his dog immediately after getting up in the morning. The dog welcomes him joyfully. Generally, the dog owner talks to his dog, pets it, gives him a treat and often walks with him before breakfast. This close contact is maintained throughout the day.

Of course the dog's behaviours stand out. Maybe it doesn't want to go out when it rains. Maybe it always sleeps next to it's basket. Maybe it will bark at the first sound of the alarm clock. If now after the death of this dog the new dog shows the same behaviour patterns, the idea can quickly arise that the old soul was reborn in the new dog.

But what about a rabbit, a guinea pig, a snake or a bird? Every animal has its characteristics, but in case of those just mentioned, they are simply less noticeable than in dogs or cats. In only a few cases are there extremely conspicuous behaviour patterns in these animals which suggest that the new animal is the rebirth of the old one.

If you, dear reader, have loved your animal and this animal was happy with you, it will try to come back to you, no matter if it is a dog, a horse, a turtle or another animal.

To protect privacy, I have partially changed the names of people and places.

Contents

INTRODUCTION

We think that humans are the crowning glory of creation, they have a soul. We think it is possible that the soul of humans will come to paradise or be born again. In the meantime, many also concede a soul to animals. Can the soul of an animal also come to paradise or be reborn?

Can a human soul be reborn as an animal? Or would this be a descent from the precious soul of humans to the low soul level of an animal? Is the level of the human soul really higher than the soul level of an animal? How do we know, or better believe we know, that humans are the higher soul being and, for example, the dog is the lower soul being?

The religions that know reincarnation agree that life is about learning love. It is about the development of human towards love and when it comes to love, the dog is far superior to us humans, because the dog loves us more than himself.

Maybe it is time for us humans to rethink our views.

Maybe this will create a completely different view of the world.

"If there are no dogs in Heaven, then when I die I want to go where they went."
Will Rogers

MY DOGS

In spring 2014 my book "Krebs bei Hunden erfolgreich behandeln" (successful treatment of cancer in dogs) was published, in which I also report about my dogs and my relationship to them.

I write that I believe that our Labrador Asko was the rebirth of our previous dog Charly. Interestingly, no one has mocked me because of this thesis. On the contrary, I received emails and letters from people telling me their stories and thoughts about reincarnation, rebirth and transmigration. I will publish the most interesting of them in this book, but first of all the capital from my book that triggered these reactions.

Heinz Rühmann (a German actor) said: "You can live without a dog, but it's not worth it".

I agree. I love dogs and have had a dog at my side almost all the time since I was three years old. The first dog of our family was a black and white Cocker Spaniel, we called her Corny, a very beautiful animal. Her breeder sometimes picked her up here to present her at shows.

Corny was actually a nightmare. She jumped into every puddle and rolled around in things you don't like, fresh cow pats were very popular. She was stubborn, greedy and had a very memorable sense of obedi-

ence, but she was also cuddly and very teachable. No dog could do so many tricks. So every morning, when we let her into the garden, she brought the daily newspaper from the mailbox without being asked, afterwards there were treats. On Sundays we got no newspaper, so there was no treat. One Sunday morning Corny brought a dirty newspaper page with her, which she had taken out of the compost and from then on she knew how to get a reward on Sunday regardless.

When I was fifteen, my parents were in hospital at the same time, mother due to an accident and father with a heart attack. I was staying with friends. When I returned home, Corny had disappeared. My parents never told me what had happened to her. The pain of losing my dog is still present when I think about it.

A year later I got a dog called Lumpi from my friend, who had to go to hospital. Lumpi was an incredible mixture of Afghan and Rottweiler, an extremely impressive animal, tall, blond, long-haired and with a catastrophic urge for freedom. My friend Charly lived in Mardorf at the Steinhuder Meer (German lake) and Lumpi was "allowed" to run around freely on the property and the adjoining forest. Of course this was not possible in our village. As much as we took care, Lumpi was always gone.

We had the dog for two years and three times he has run the twenty-five miles back to Mardorf. The third time, a neighbour of my friend, who had died in the meantime, suggested that he would take the dog. Due to the fact that they were dog lovers and the dog had more freedom, our family agreed with a heavy heart. When Lumpi was no longer with us, my father cried and said that there would never be another dog in his house again. After that my father was very sad. He missed the dog, the daily walk, the conversation with other dog owners and last but not least the affection and love that Lumpi had brought into his life.

A few months later I worked in Minden on a construction site right next to an animal shelter. At lunchtime I visited it to look at the dogs. The day before a puppy had been brought, someone had rescued it from the Weser (river), about three months old and playful to full. After work I called my father and asked him to pick me up from the construction site, I told him nothing about the dog.

When he arrived, I was standing in front of the animal shelter with the manager of the shelter and the puppy. Father grasped the situation immediately, got out of the car and began to scold: „What are you doing!" No way he wanted a new dog, he still had enough of the last one and so on. I expected this reaction and explained the situation to the manager of the shelter in advance. In the middle of my father's speech she suddenly said "Hold this" and put the puppy into his hands. Father said nothing more, he looked at the puppy and said: "Okay, let's go home".

We named the dog Charly after my late friend.

It was an absolute super-dog, a Spitz cross, full-grown he had 16 inches shoulder height. He had only positive qualities and was extremely affectionate. We had a huge apple tree in the garden at that time. In autumn I put a ladder to the tree to pick the apples in the crown. I climbed into the tree and after a short time an anxious howl sounded right next to me. Charly had climbed up the ladder and now clung to two rungs about twelve feet above the ground. He trembled with fear. I couldn't go down the ladder because the dog was hanging there. I was also worried that he might fall down. I called for my wife, but she didn't hear me in the house. After a felt eternity, our neighbour Klaus appeared and carefully climbed up the ladder and brought the dog safely back to the ground. I was still in the tree, but as soon as I was back on the ladder Charly tried to climb the ladder again. On the third attempt Klaus picked him down again.

At the age of sixteen, Charly lost his hearing and we switched him to sign language, he still followed excellent. We were able to let him run free as usual. Every fifteen feet he turned around. If we wanted something from him, we only had to hold one arm up, then he stopped waiting for further instructions. Should he come, I had to turn around, should he stay, I had to show a palm as a stop signal. We and the other dog owners in the village had a lot of fun because of this *special situation. Charly became over eighteen years old. We had him put to sleep when he went blind.*

What I'm writing now, some of you will find strange and others even quaint, but it's true. Since my childhood I have been interested in religion, especially Buddhism. I am enthusiastic about the idea of rebirth, yes, I believe in it, just like almost half of the world's population. Our Charly was a great dog, a picture book dog, I wanted him back, but how do you find a dog that was reborn? Chance or Providence is supposed to fix something like that.

After about six months I was looking for a puppy. Half a year I waited, so that Charly could be reborn in a different way. Stop grinning, I mean it seriously.

One day my mother came home from work and brought a daily newspaper from Bielefeld (50 miles from our place of residence) which she had just received by chance. In this newspaper there was only one ad under the heading "Sales Animals", "Labrador Puppies for Sale". We phoned, made an appointment and on the weekend we drove all together to Bielefeld.

Eight black Labrador puppies, three months old, were waiting for us, one of them immediately came running to me and chewed on my shoelaces. Then he went to my mother and bit her little toe. This cheeky puppie became our new dog.

My father couldn't take the idea that the spirit of our Charly should be in this dog serious and my mother always thought everything was impossible anyway.

The dog was called Asko. When we brought him to his new home, he was thrilled. There was so much to discover. He romped through the garden, crawling into every corner and examining his new basket in the winter garden. There was only one place in the whole garden that he avoided and always avoided and that was the kennel. This hut of massive beech had always been the refuge of all our dogs. Charly, our last dog, also liked to use it for years. But about two years earlier something had happened and since then Charly had not entered the kennel and had not gone near it.

We came back from holiday and Charly ran happily through his garden, went into his hut and immediately came running to me howling with a bleeding nose. A big cat had made himself comfortable in the hut during our absence and had given our dog three bleeding wounds with a paw stroke when he stuck his nose in it.

Now Asko also avoided this hut, you can see that as proof of a rebirth, I don't know. Judge for yourself.

Asko developed into an absolute super dog, he had no character weaknesses. He was in no way inferior to our Charly. If I had to give him a certificate, I would write: Asko fulfilled the expectations placed in him to our complete satisfaction.

At the age of seven, Asko fell ill with osteoarthritis. A short time later he developed a neurological disease from one day to the next. Now he was always very sad when he was alone. My wife and I decided to buy a second dog. My parents were no longer alive at this time.

At that time I was enthusiastic about sledge dog racing. I went to many events, did a musher course and spent a holiday on a sledge dog tour. The sledge dog virus had gripped me. It was supposed to be a sledge dog. So we came to our present dog, an Akita Inu with some Malamut share. Kita was one and a half years old and already trained as a sledge dog when she came to us. She got along with Asko immediately and Asko really blossomed again. That was the best decision we could make.

Two years later we put Asko to sleep. He was only nine years old, but I didn't want to put him through the pain and medication. Kita is now almost fourteen years old and in good health. For five years I was doing dog sledding with her, then I became ill, cancer. Now I am healthy again, but the dog is too old and maybe I am too.

Why am I telling you all this? I want to express that I know what it means to "own" a dog. I know how hard it is to say goodbye when the time has come, but I also know what it means to have to say goodbye to a dog even though the time has not yet come.

When you adopt a dog, you have a lot of very good days and one very bad day."

W. Bruce Cameron

BRUNO AND BIFF

This letter reached me shortly after the publication of my book "Successful Treatment of Cancer in Dogs". I shortened the letter because it is probably not interesting for you as a reader why Mrs Winter became aware of me and my book. I also omitted the further thoughts about rebirth, death and God because they were very personal.

Do you believe in transmigration? Well, I do. In November 2002 we had to put our beloved Biff to sleep. He was 14 years old, a mixed male, weighed 24 lbs and had only three legs. He lost his left hind leg in an accident when he was one year old.

In summer 2003 we got another puppy. Also a mixed breed, because they are healthier and have more individuality. Bruno grew up. He resembled our deceased Biff in many ways and had some behaviour from him. At that time we still believed that this was due to the circumstances.

So Bruno came just like Biff used to in the morning, when our alarm clock rang from its basket in the hallway up the stairs and sat down in front of our bedroom door to start the day together with us. He also loved to eat pears. After one year the unbelievable happened. Bruno no longer walked on his left hind leg. Like his predecessor Biff, he ran on three legs. Of course we went to the vet. He couldn't find anything and said that it was probably a sprain that would regenerate itself.

But Bruno continued to walk on three paws and seemed to have no pain. After about half a year my husband had a totally crazy idea. He gave Bruno a bandage on his right hind leg, just to see what was happening. And what happened? Bruno continued running on three legs, but now he held up the wrapped leg! So he ran on the supposedly ill one. For us this was proof that everything had to be in order with his left leg, otherwise Bruno wouldn't be able to burden it.

Bruno is now eleven years old and has been walking on three legs for ten years. If Bruno dies one day, we will not mourn him for a second, because we know that he will come back. However, we hope that next time he will walk with us on four paws. He doesn't have to prove anything to us anymore.

A member of an esoteric forum reports that his tomcat had broken his pelvis when it jumped from the second floor at the age of one. Since then it always had to stretch his right hind leg forward while sitting. The tomcat died at the age of twelve.

Two years later the scribe fetched two young tom-cats, one optically the exact image of the deceased. It often stretches the right hind leg forward while sitting, just like the deceased tomcat did. There are also photos and videos available.

An interview with Richard Gere appeared in the Bildzeitung in 2009. He is a Buddhist and answered the question whether dogs can be reborn: "Of course, everything is energy, everything flows."

ALANKA BECAME ARKO

I print the following letter in the original wording. Judge for yourself.

We live in F. a small village near H. Five years ago, our Alanka was run over by a timber truck on a forest road. We were in deep sorrow, she was only three years old. We never wanted a dog again, because every dog dies one day and we didn't want to experience that again.

Life went on without a dog, but of course we never forgot Alanka. In summer 2013 we moved because our rented house was sold, but we stayed in the village, four streets further in a ground floor flat.

Then we were on holiday in Turkey. A woman asked us if we could take a dog with us on the return flight. The dog was a young stray dog and has been caught on the beach. We should only take him with us to Germany so that he can be conveyed. Because it didn't cost us anything, we said yes. The dog had to be locked into a box and we felt sorry for him, but it should lead for him into a better future.

In Germany we picked him up with someone from this organization in the baggage claim area. At that moment we decided to keep him. We donated 350 Euro and could keep him. Our son picked us up and something strange happened. When the dog, we didn't even have a name for it, saw our son coming from afar, he whimpered with joy. He didn't know our son. Hundreds of people were running around, but he only had eyes for him, jumped up on him and was happy. Now we had to explain some things, but our son loved to have a dog in the house again.

All four of us were happy and drove home. On the way we stopped every ten miles because the dog had diarrhoea. We took short walks and noticed that Arko, as we called him in the meantime, obeyed very well. He never went further than fifteen feet away from us and then we were so brave and even let him run without a leash.

Two hours later we were home. Arko jumped out, ran down the street and was gone. Our son immediately searches for him by car, but he didn't find Arko. We asked our neighbours to help us find him. It is a small village, everyone knows each other and we help each other. I don't know who searched with us, at least we found Arko. He was sitting on the doorstep of the house that we lived in when our Alanka was still alive. He was very happy to see us, but wanted to go into this house. The new owner was not at home. We put a leash on Arko and brought him to our flat.

Now everyone can think what they want. Maybe it was a confusion with a lot of coincidence or something else, but that was not all. Arko is now with us for two years. He follows me at every turn, obeying my word. I can take him everywhere, into the city, into the forest, everywhere but not on the forest road on which our Alanka was run over five years ago. Me, my wife and my son know very well that Arko has the soul of Alanka.

WINGED CATS

In spring 2010, when I had just published the book about my own cancer, I met a somewhat peculiar woman around fifty years old at the Steinhuder Meer (German lake). I call her Mrs May, in line with the month I met her.

She told me that she lives with her cats nearby in a lonely house. Two of the cats have wings, but of course they couldn't fly and one would not fly anyway because one of the wings had fallen off. Dramatic, not the fallen wing, but the woman who seemed to be a little bit crazy.

However, she seemed extremely sensible to me in the further conversation. We talked about simple, self-determined life, self-sufficiency and the likes and also about the book "Walden" by H.D. Thoreau. I had read the book decades ago and found it extremely interesting.

"Thoreau had a neighbour, who also had a winged cat, is written in the book by the way," Mrs May told me. "Winged cats were much more common at that time than they are today, there are hardly any left and if you tell someone that you have one, you are immediately looked at as if you are crazy."

At home I took the book from the shelf and searched unsuccessfully for the mention of winged cats. So I searched the internet and what did I find? Photos of winged cats, old photos, new photos, newspaper reports, scientific explanations, there were and there are winged cats! A few days later I visited my new acquaintance and looked at her two animals. It was spooky, because one cat even shimmered greenish and both had wings. Everything was exactly as Mrs May had described it.

Wing is not quite the right word, because these wings have no feathers, they are rather skin and cartilage appendages. It looks like two hairy "wings" about ten inches long growing out of the spine to the left and right at shoulder level. These are not connected to the bone structure or the muscle system. They are skin growths as far as I can judge. At the base, where the wing is connected to the skin, it has a thickness of about 1 x 0.4 inches. The connection to the skin, however, is only as big as a one-cent coin, so overall a rather fragile affair. The wings cannot be moved. Depending on how the cats stand or sit, they either hang down sideways or lie on their backs. They are very flexible, which you can see when the cats roll around.

I'm a very curious person, trying to fathom everything. So also this time. I started researching the internet and after a few hours I found a man in southern Germany who pretended to be an expert for winged cats. I called him and described the problem that my friend's cat had lost a wing, which was true and asked him what to do. It soon turned out that the man himself had a winged cat, but he was certainly not an expert, at least not for winged cats.

So I continued my search on the internet and came across a woman, whom I assumed due to various statements that she also had a winged cat. I talked to her on the phone, she was a veterinarian. I told her about my experience, the book I had written, it was a very nice conversation. Then we talked about the cats and she said that she thinks that you can make any cat grow wings. However, she considered this to be cruelty to animals and so she would not reveal her knowledge.

As I said, I am very curious and passionate about research. Within a few days I found out why these malformations can occur. In principle, it is a mild, but permanent poisoning caused by contaminated drinking water.

Mrs May has a very different explanation, however:

In the summer of 1995, after a storm, Mrs May went into the forest to get a thick branch that had broken off an oak tree. Right next to the branch lay an adult dead little owl. She heard strangely lamenting sounds, followed the noises and found a large now open cave with two young little owls at a height of about six feet where the branch had broken off. The two lay unprotected in the sun.

Mrs May took off her jacket, put two pieces of wood through her sleeves and arranged the whole thing to make a roof with an entrance hole. Then she went with her wheelbarrow so far away that she could barely see the nest, sat down in the cart and waited to see if the second adult bird would take care of the young.

When nothing had happened after two hours, she went looking for worms and brought them to the chicks. They didn't let themselves be asked for long. As she lifted the jacket, they both ripped open their beaks and Mrs May let worm after worm slide in. Then she went to a rotten tree trunk and looked for maggots that were also eaten greedily.

Since no adult bird could be seen over the course of several hours, Mrs May decided to take the two chicks and the dead adult bird home with her. There she packed the dead little owl in a plastic bag and put it in the freezer. Private individuals are not allowed to keep protected animals. Mrs May should have informed the district forester or another authority. Since she did not intend to hand over the chicks, but did not want to be a nest robber, she kept the dead parent bird as proof.

Mrs May's house is a small old farmhouse with an adjoining barn. In the gable of the barn a small window is walled in. Mrs May took out the window wing and in front of it she placed a large old wooden box, into which she had previously sawn a hole at the height of the window. The new cave was ready, with a lid to open at the top.

The chicks already had their first feathers, so it wouldn't be long before they grew up. In the compost there were enough earthworms to feed them all the time. Later, Mrs May also caught mice with a mousetrap and watched enthusiastically as her little owls divided them. Time passed and both chicks had grown into beautiful little owls, but they did not want to leave their cave. The food was good, in the meantime they were also fed with small cut cattle hearts and similar from the butcher. The cave was also regularly cleaned. In the following spring the two were still sitting in their hotel with full board.

It couldn't go on like this. First Mrs May fed less and then no more at all, but the two were so well nourished that it took them a week until they made efforts to fly. Both sat on the windowsill and looked down at Mrs May as she walked across the courtyard. What should she do, she couldn't teach them how to fly. So she laid a few live worms and cut cattle hearts on the meadow, sat next to it and waited. It worked, both owls came flying to eat. Then they flew together up an apple tree and later back into their box.

That's how it went for nine years. The two never hunted themselves, they stayed with Mrs May all their lives. During the day they both liked to sit on the roof of the chicken coop and watch Mrs May working in the garden, doing her laundry or sitting in the sun. During the breeding season the little owls were always surrounded by noisy small birds, which they wanted to drive away, but that didn't interest them at all.

Mrs May had the impression that they both wanted to come into the house, however she didn't want to start that as well. At the age of nine, the little owls died of old age within a few days. They were buried in the garden under a rose bush.

Half a year later two young cats appeared at Mrs May's house, she discovered them in the barn. The two were sitting on the wooden box, which was still standing in front of the window. Mrs May first got a huge shock because she thought she saw her two "little owls" in the back light. She thought they were ghosts. An adult little owl is about ten inches tall, the size of a young cat, and its silhouette is also very similar.

About a year later the two cats started "wing growth" at the same time.

Mrs May is convinced that her two little owls have been reborn as cats to live very closely with her now and they are allowed to do so. Meanwhile there are other cats living on the farm. None of the other cats has formed wings, although all eat and drink the same. So either it's not true that water poisoning makes the wings grow or the other cats are immune. Or Mrs May is right in claiming that the two cats are her reborn little owls who want to show with their wings that they really are.

The whole thing is strange anyway. When I started writing this book in spring 2015, I went to Mrs May with the text you just read to get her permission to publish it. The two winged cats were sitting on the roof of the chicken coop, just as Mrs May had described to me from her little owls. In the meantime the one fallen wing had re-grown, but it is only four inches long.

I would like to say something very important about Mrs May. She lives this isolated self-determined life because she is afraid of her fellow human beings because of her experiences

I wrote at the beginning that I thought she was a little crazy. I don't think so anymore. Mrs May has managed to lead an independent self-sufficient life for over twenty years. She has never taken advantage of state support. From morning till evening she works on her farm, where she lives completely alone. She plants and harvests and what she has too much, she sells to friends in order to pay electricity, water and property taxes with this money. My respect to Mrs May.

"There are no more pyres. Today nobody gets burned any more. We are humane and civilized. If someone has other thoughts, acts differently, has a different view, he is no longer put before a farmer's court with torches and pitchforks. Today we have completely different possibilities, internet, Facebook and so on. Sometimes I think that the funeral pyre was the more human solution."
Mrs May

The scientific explanation:

Cats that grow wings have a genetic skin disease called Feline Kutanasthenia. With this disease, the cat's skin becomes extremely elastic around the shoulders and so in some rare cases it can lead to these wing-like outgrowths.

If you would like to go deeper into the topic, you will find good information on the side messybeast.com, filled with winged cat pictures. It is said that almost every cat carries the predisposition to this genetic skin disease, which can break out due to an extreme malnutrition.

Is this explanation the disenchantment of history? No, absolutely not. There is this disease, but it is not clear why two young cats, which later grow wings, appear with Mrs May and take there the places of the deceased little owls.

KNOWLEDGE

If you knew exactly that you are always right in 51% of all cases, you could earn millions every day at the stock exchange. You could live either in the sunny south on a private island or in a penthouse in a city with a huge cultural offer.

All this because you are right in only 51% of all cases. Well, you know it is not and because you are not even right in 51% of cases, you should never claim that others are wrong on issues where there are different opinions.

You can say, I do not believe in acupuncture, then that is your opinion, but to say that acupuncture does not help is completely unfounded.

If you don't believe in soul migration, that's up to you, but to claim that there is no soul migration is like swearing that there are no winged cats just because you've never seen any.

DOG LOVERS ARE DIFFERENT – CAT LOVERS TOO

While researching for this book, I noticed something strange. Most of the stories about reincarnated dogs were told to me orally, quite differently in the case of reborn cats. Here I was contacted almost exclusively by email. If I wanted to ask more details and asked for a phone call, I rarely got it, but emails were always answered. With the dog owners it was exactly the other way round. If I had sent an email with a question, I often got the phone number to call.

Cat owners write, dog owners talk. My guess: The dog owner has to go outside with his dog several times a day. There he meets other people, often dog owners as well and then they talk. Cat owners usually live with their pet inside the building, which they do not have to leave because of the animal. Thus they have also no points of contact with other cat owners and are therefore more active in the internet. It may be that I am wrong, but I do not have another explanation.

IRIS BERBEN

Iris Berben is extraordinary fascinating German actress.

In a 2006 issue of the magazine "Dogs", Mrs Berben raves about her dog Paul, a Jack Russell male:

"I think he understands everything. I once shed quiet tears. There comes this dog, puts his snout on my cheek and comforts me. Paul has deep emotions from sadness to joy. He can even laugh heartily. For me he is the reincarnation of Buster Keaton. He has this sad melancholy. He wants to tell me: "The literature you love so much, Iris, is not alien to me." Our emotional worlds are not far apart."

MRS KLEIN AND HER CAT

The following story was told to me by Mrs Klein from Hanover. I wrote it down after our conversation and read it to her. Mrs Klein added the last paragraph. She is happy that her story will be published because she has seen a lot of suffering in her professional life. She often had to deliver the news that someone had died. She knows how much bereaved people suffer and hopes to alleviate the suffering of a few people by publishing her story.

My sixteenth birthday was the worst day of my life. We lived in Silesia. It was the SecondWorld War. The enemy came closer and we had to leave our beloved homeland. We fled on the loading area of a coal truck and could only take some clothes and food with us.

We had a cat and that for as long as I could remember. Mischka was always with me. When I was one year old, my parents took me to a photographer in town to capture my first birthday. In the photo I still have, I am standing next to a chair and Mischka is sitting on it.

When we escaped, we left our animals behind. We had eight chickens, two pigs and of course the old Mischka. We let our animals go because nobody knew exactly what was going to happen. We buried valuables that we could not take with us in the vegetable garden. Our bicycles were hidden in the forest. When we fled we believed that the war would soon be over and that we could just return home. Now, as everyone knows, things were different.

My escape ended in Bochum, in the Ruhr area. As a refugee it was not easy. My family was forcibly housed. A stroke of luck for me, because thanks to the relationship of the gentleman I was able to train as a nurse. Over the years I became a surgical nurse and when my boss went to South Africa he caught up with me.

I have seen a lot of the world. I lived in Australia, India, Venezuela, Japan and the USA. I never got married or built a long-term relationship with anyone. Most of the time I was in one place for only one or two years, then I moved on again. I was very good at my job as surgical nurse and had excellent grades.

I retired when I was 64. My girlfriend, we still knew each other from Silesia, lived in Hannover and so I moved there too. On my 66th birthday my neighbour asked me if I would like to have a kitten? Her cat had kittens, now so old that they should be given away.

No, I didn't want a cat, however I wanted to have a look at the litter. In the evening I went to my neighbour and what happened next, I can hardly describe.

The mother cat was lying on the side under the heater. Little kittens lay close to her. You couldn't tell how many there were. My eyes were magic-ally attracted to a kitten. It was the second from the left. Actually only the back was to be seen. I sat down on the floor and began to stroke this kit-ten. Then it lifted its head and I thought the blow was hitting me.

It was my Mischka. My cat, which I had left ex-actly fifty years ago to the day, now lay in front of me. Like Mischka, this kitten had a two-coloured nose, and that wasn't all. It was a feeling deep in-side me. I suddenly knew it was Mischka. I knew it without any doubt. Of course I kept the kitten and called her Mischka, another name would not have been possible, because she was Mischka.

One year later I went to my neighbour and showed her the photo from my first birthday, where Mischka 1 can also be seen. At this time Mischka 1 must have been one year old like now Mischka 2. Both cats are striped and they were alike as Tweedledum and Tweedledee. It looks like it is the same cat. It's not the same cat, that's clear, but it's the same soul, I'm firmly convinced of that.

I never thought about what would happen after death. My thoughts were for the living. Now I know what comes next, it goes on. The soul is immortal. My soul as well as the soul of every animal. And not only that, perhaps the soul can decide freely when and where it wants to go in the next life. That's the only way to explain that Mischka has come back to me. If Mischka had come to me earlier, I probably would not have seen her at all, because I lived only for my work. Nor would I have had time for her. She came at just the right time. Her little soul must have planned it that way. Maybe she observed me for fifty years waiting for the right moment. Fifty years are a long time, but if the soul is immortal, fifty years are nothing more than a blink of an eye for a soul.

I have seen the photo from the first birthday of Mrs Klein and Mischka 1. Also a photo of Mischka 2 at the age of two. Both cats are striped, the patterns are 100% identical. They actually were alike as Tweedledum and Tweedledee.

In the eyes of my cat lies a greater mystery than in a fleeing galaxy.
René Thom

BLACKY THE WHITE TOMCAT THAT DISSAPEARED WITHOUT TRACE

A young woman from my cancer support group told me this story. She has experienced it.

My father had a black tomcat. Blacky had come to my family years before me. Daddy loved this animal, I felt it somehow scary. I don't know why. Blacky died at the age of twenty. One day he was just dead. Dad was sad, and didn't want to have a pet anymore.

My father was an architect, very down-to-earth, very quiet, very silent and extremely fanciless. He designed industrial complexes. Functionality was my father's world, both professionally and privately. He was a very good father to me, everything always ran smoothly. There were no ups and downs. Jokes made daddy only at Christmas and problems were solved without much fuss. I have to describe my father here, so that one can understand the further.

About a year after Blacky died, Dad called from the road. He was on the way back from Berlin and at a rest area a cat had jumped into his open car. Dad was totally excited, he said: "That's impossible. He looks just like Blacky. I'll bring him along."

Three hours later, my father walked in at the door, beaming with happiness. He carried the cat on his arm and scratched it. My mother and me looked at each other blankly. This cat was white grey tabby. There was none, really not the slightest resemblance to Blacky. Blacky was tall and strong, this tomcat was dainty. He weighed at most half of Blacky. Dad put him on the carpet and himself beside it. "Isn't that incredible?" he asked. "Isn't this resemblance incredible?" I would have believed any other person to be joking, not Daddy. At first I thought he had gone crazy, but that is very unlike him. "Daddy" I said "Blacky was black, this cat is white grey." Dad looked at me, then at the tomcat and said: "So what, then he's just white." I think he didn't realize until that moment that he had seen something that corresponded to a wishful thinking. My father never spoke about his error again.

The tomcat was called Blacky. A rather silly name for a white grey tabby cat. Blacky got used to us immediately, he walked around the house and regarded us as his staff. At night he slept on Daddy's bedside table just like his predecessor. Otherwise he had exactly the same behaviour as the original Blacky, with one difference. This tomcat never left the house in ten years. He wasn't even in the garden, he never even took a step outside the door. When we went on holiday, he stayed at home and was taken care of by a neighbour. We could have taken him with us, we wanted to, but he didn't.

At the age of 55, Dad had a severe heart attack and retired. He read a lot, watched TV and kept fit with his trimming bike. Blacky was always with him. Two years later, it was a Sunday in November, my father died of another heart attack. He died the way he had lived, unspectacular. In the morning he straightened up in bed, grabbed his heart, fell back again and that was it. We called the doctor, and he could only determine death.

When the doctor left the house, we noticed that Blacky was no longer in the bedroom. Most recently he was sitting next to Dad when the doctor issued the death certificate. At first we didn't attach any importance to it, we had other problems and didn't look for him. The undertaker came in the afternoon, then we looked for Blacky, but we didn't find him. We can almost exclude that he somehow got out the door. We would have seen that. We looked everywhere in the house. Blacky disappeared. Suddenly my mother became as white as chalk. She said, "He's in the coffin." We immediately called the undertaker, of course he wasn't in the coffin. How could he have gotten in there? The undertaker said that he and his coworker had not seen a tomcat with us.

Blacky never showed up again. There are three possibilities what we think could have happened.

Option number one:
He somehow left the house, but we don't believe that. It was a cold November day, all windows were closed and the front door was only opened for the doctor and the undertaker. Besides, Blacky hadn't even left the house in ten years.

Second possibility:
Blacky just vanished into thin air.

Third possibility:
Blacky committed suicide. Our house is heated with a large solid fuel boiler in the basement, extremely modern with heat storage and heat recovery. Daddy designed it. When Daddy fell over, my mum screamed for help. At this time I was in the cellar, had opened the combustion chamber door and had thrown large logs into it. I dropped everything and ran up the stairs. All the doors were open, including the door to the combustion chamber. Blacky must have run into the basement after Daddy's death and jumped into the roaring hot fire.

I hold on to this version. I have to hold on to it, otherwise I'll go crazy.

My opinion:

Suicide of a cat, is there such a thing? Suicide is an extremely complex process. The futility of one's own life must be recognized. Furthermore, there must be the knowledge that one's own death ends senselessness. In addition, in this case the decision must be made to jump into a fire. Can an animal have such complex thought processes? Can an animal think several moves in advance and coordinate its behaviour?

I don't know, but I think it is possible. In the book "Auch Tiere haben eine Seele" (Even animals have souls) by Stefano Apuzzo and Monica D'Ambrosio there is the following story of a dog who committed suicide.

Mr. Harold Myers from Texas was sent into the Vietnam War. His seven-year-old shepherd dog remained sadly at home. He waited for the return of his beloved master. One day the dog went to a nearby railway line and lay down on the tracks. Evidently he wanted to die. Several times he was rescued by passers-by. At some point nobody was there and the dog was killed by the train. A few days later the news arrived that his master had died in Vietnam.

Did the dog feel that? Did he want to follow his master by putting an end to his life? Does the dog know that he has an immortal soul? Can a tomcat out of love make the decision to jump into a fire, to burn in order to be reunited with his beloved human?

My uncle, who owned a farm, told me about the suicide of a cow. This cow was taken away from her calf. For several days she grieved for her child. This is normal, mother cows feel a pain of separation. Everyone calls for her calf for a while.

One evening my uncle fetched his cows from the pasture, Olga, yes, every cow had a name, as usual it was the first. She trotted towards the stable. About a hundred yards before the stable she began to get faster. My uncle wanted to stop her, but she ran madly towards the stable. She didn't run into the stable, but against the wall. She died immediately. And there are still people who claim that animals have no feelings.

It is only with the heart that one can see rightly; what is essential is invisible to the eye.
From „The Little Prince" Antoine de Saint-Exupéry

IN RUSSIAN CAPTIVITY

One of my sports buddies is a hobby historian. He copied the following section from the book "In Russian Captivity". The book was published in 1960.

I've been on the Eastern Front for over a year now. We were surrounded. A return to the family was out of question. One night I was woken up by dog barking. I believed that my dog Rex was there. On the other hand I thought it was impossible. Nevertheless I left the trench, crawling through the dirt past the dead towards the barking dog. Then I saw it, my dog a hundred yards away, several thousand miles from home. I called it, it jumped up and retreated. I tried to follow it in the rain and mud. Suddenly I heard a plane, a low-flying aircraft and immediately deafening noise, machine gun fire, explosions, screams. The trench in which I had lain before was a grave, I was the only survivor.

This is the descriptions of Michael Hirt. When he came home years later, he was told that his dog had died about the date it appeared to him.

Our perfect companions never have fewer than four feet."
Colette

YOUTUBE

On YouTube you can see a video showing an old man walking along the lake with a white cat. Then the cat runs towards the water and comes back with a thin stick, about twenty inches long, which it places in front of the man's feet. He grabs the stick, the cat runs around him several times and runs to the lake. He throws the stick about ten yards into the water. The cat jumps after it with a dive, fetches the stick, brings it back and immediately runs towards the lake again. The same game repeats itself a few more times. The story behind tells Robert from Arkansas, the man in the video.

He had a black Labrador for eleven years, with which he went every day to the lake to play. Every day, as he emphasizes: "Every day! Every fucking day!" When his dog died, he and his wife decided to buy a cat because Robert couldn't walk well since a hip operation. It took them almost a year to find a white tomcat they liked.

When Robert led the cat to the lake with a leash and collar for the first time, the tomcat brought a stick and was keen to play. Robert says that for a moment he even thought he heard his dog barking. So now Robert has a tomcat who, like his dog, insists on playing at the lake every day. "Every day! Every fucking day!"

The last sentence in the rather lengthy video is: "This is my dog, nothing else. It's him, you can crucify me if he's not."

THE HOAX OF THE RABBIT RISEN FROM THE DEAD

How true are stories from the internet? The following story has been haunting the web for years. I have found it in four different variations, including a Sailor, a Bicycle and a New Zealand forum. I don't know if it ever happened.

Here's the shortest version.

The brother of my colleague was invited to a friend's birthday party, it was barbecued. A couple had their dog with them, which was running around in the garden. At some point the dog had something in his mouth and licked it. It was a dead white rabbit. The rabbit belonged to the neighbour, he kept it in an open enclosure on his property. The dog must have taken it from there.

What to do? To avoid quarrels, they took the rabbit, washed it clean, dried it and threw it over the fence back into its enclosure. The next day the rabbit owner stood at the fence stunned and reported that his rabbit had died yesterday, that he had buried it and that it was now lying in his enclosure again.

Like I said, a hoax. In such stories it is usually the case that it happened to a friend of a friend. They rarely mention names or places. In this case neither rabbit nor dog nor the neighbour have a name.

There is also the story of the newly bought yucca palm from which at home a tarantula crawled, happened to the girlfriend of an aunt or another third or fourth person. There is a lot of rubbish on the internet, that is well known. During my research on the web I tried to find only true stories. I don't know whether I succeeded or not. If I found a story in two different versions, I thought it was either invented or strongly changed.

I'm also very sceptical if the animals don't have a name. If this was the case, I checked who the author of the article is, how long he has been registered in the forum, how many posts he had written and what else he reported about. For example, if someone has been active in an animal forum for years, reporting about his animal, telling that it has become ill, died afterwards and then claims after a while that it has now come back as a rebirth, then I believe him.

Attention, watch out! I believe him. So I believe that he sees it, feels it and is convinced of it, but it does not mean that I believe the story. There can always be a lot of wishful thinking and imagination. I don't even know what to think about some of the stories in this book.

Decide for yourself what you believe.

JACKIE THE HARE

In a forum about animal communication and energetics I found a report by a woman from Berlin.

Her hare Jackie died of a stroke. She had telepathic contact with it after its death further and got so the info that it would reincarnate in the spring 2015. The woman found her Jackie again. It was born in May 2015 at the same breeder and it looked just like before. She writes that she had agreed on a sign and in fact it knew the sign. Jackie recognized its old toys, its little house and its hare friends.

It makes no difference whether a human being or animal lives or not. A contact to the soul is established independently of the body. The soul is always present. It is immortal, infinite and omnipresent.
The Healer

QUOTE: THE HEALER

"When you engage with the themes of energetic healing, distance healing and transmigration, you will see nothing like others see it, because you see it the way you see and understand it thanks to your changed perception. You know things that most others don't because you know things that others aren't willing to know and that they will never be able to understand. You know that there is a knowledge that is accessible only to those who know that there are things worth knowing about which they know nothing.

What you know and what others know is so different that your knowledge cannot be added to the knowledge of others. Your knowledge cannot supplement or enrich the knowledge of others, because the knowledge or ignorance of others excludes it."

MY LADY DOG KITA

My dog was treated by the healer whose quote you will find on page 57.

When Kita was about ten years old, she became incontinent. As a young dog she was spayed and a side effect of this measure is often age incontinence in large breeds. We tried it with different homeopathic remedies, nothing helped. So we laid out transparent plastic underlays in our house at all favourite places of our Kita. Not nice, but not changeable, we thought.

Through my support group I came into contact with a healer who works exclusively with distance healing. He helped a woman from my group with her cancer and depression.

During a conversation I mentioned the incontinence of our Kita and the healer suggested a remote treatment. He got a photo of our dog with about twenty hairs of it, stuck on the back with sellotape.

Two days later our dog was cured, no more traces of incontinence. For almost a year Kita was daily, sometimes several times incontinent and now after only two treatments this was over.

After about two weeks I wanted to remove the plastic underlays, because I thought they were superfluous. However, my wife said that she did not trust the whole thing and so the underlays remained. On the same evening our dog was incontinent again for the first time and also several times the next day. I called the healer and asked for an explanation. He said that my wife had destroyed the energetic field with her mistrust. He did two after-treatments, after which Kita was "not leaking" again.

Today there is only one single plastic sheet left in our flat, where Kita lies after the walk. If you now think that I can give you an explanation, I have to disappoint you. I absolutely do not understand what is going on. There are theories, experiments, speculations, scientific studies, etc. on this subject, but is that important? It is essential that we and our dog have been helped. How is irrelevant. I don't have the slightest idea how my computer works, I'm satisfied that I can use it.

READING IN CAT FORUMS

In a cat forum a woman writes that she lost her cat Happy in August 2009 to an animal-hater. The successor is called Spencer and she is convinced that Spencer is the rebirth of her deceased Happy. She tells us that Spencer, for example, only plays with toys that Happy has played with and he has exactly the same quirks as Happy.

Both cats also have some particularly conspicuous and strange habits. Every time the owner went to the toilet, Happy went along and put itself in her pants and that's exactly what Spencer does. When she sniffs her nose, Spencer gets its crazy five minutes, just like Happy before. She also writes that there are many other things, but looking into Spencer's eyes she knows it's Happy.

Elsewhere, a woman reports about an approximately six-week-old tomcat that the family found in the garden half a year after the death of their beloved cat Minka. The little cat was taken into the house and knew his way around immediately. Nothing seemed to be strange to him. The litter box was still in the same place where the little one found it immediately. The next day the husband moved the litter box to another place and little tomcat Merlin had trouble finding it. The fact that the wife had dreamed about exactly this little tomcat with the conspicuous white spot on his neck shortly before is another story.

Another great story is in the same forum. It reads fantastic. The author found his deceased cat Mucki by a dream.

At the breeder he decided to take another sister with him and named the kittens Annelie and Agnes. At home he let both of them out of the transport box, but while Agnes reacted carefully and reservedly to the new environment, Annelie was immediately at home. After only a few minutes she had taken the favourite toy of the deceased cat from its hiding place and played with it continuously. Annelie had the same ticking eye twitch as Mucki had. Furthermore she reacts on the name Mucki, the sister Agnes does not react at all. Annelie understands commands, which Mucki also knew, her sister doesn't. Mucki knew that he must not jump on the kitchen sideboard. Annelie has never jumped up there before, she avoids this place, unlike Agnes, who is always to be found there.

Other examples are given. Particularly interesting about this description is, that there are two cats of one litter, which are completely different in their behaviour. While one cat is frightened by certain typical household noises such as the bell, egg cooker, television, the other cat reacts with indifference, just like it has known these noises for years, probably it is even so.

Elsewhere I found the story of a ghost cat.

Urmeli had died in an accident in the flat at the age of six, but every family member had the feeling that the cat was still present. Leaning doors opened and a flower vase, which had been placed on Urmelis favourite spot on the windowsill, fell on the floor in the middle of the night, when everyone was in bed, clinking loudly. The favourite toy, a small colourful leather ball, disappeared without trace a few days after Urmeli's death. All family members heard a cat running through the rooms at night, just like Urmeli had always done. Friends believed to have heard the typical purring sound in the garden. And so on, it was haunted. The haunting happened every day, usually several family members were present, but nobody had an explanation what was going on.

The family brought an adult cat from the shelter. Her owner had passed away. According to the shelter, it was an extremely quiet and adaptable animal. This cat came into the house, ran a few meters into the hall, turned around and tried to get out of the front door, which was closed. It ran through the flat in panic, jumped into the living room curtains and was determined to leave the house. Mr. X caught it, put on its collar and leash and went with it into the garden, but it only wanted to leave. He left the property and the cat slowly calmed down, but refused to go back on the property. In the meantime it was too late to take it back to the shelter, so it should be put back into the transport box in the car, but the cat became completely hysterical.

Mrs X decided to take the cat to a neighbour's house overnight, also to see what would happen. There the cat curiously walked around the flat and behaved normally. The friend agreed to bring the cat back to the shelter the next day, because it shouldn't get into the family car anymore.

Family X was still longing for a new cat, but even a big stray tomcat, who was running around in the garden, did not want to enter this house. The haunting lasted two years, then it was over from one day to the next. A few months later a kitten was sitting in the garden under the Hollywood swing, a favourite spot of the late Urmeli. Where this cat came from, nobody knows. It went into the house like it had always been there. On the second day, it played in the living room with the little colourful leather ball that had been missing for two years.

Because of the events, family X decided to name the new cat Urmeli as well. The whole family is convinced that the spirit of Urmeli is back. They believe that it was always there, only during the time of conception, pregnancy, birth and baby time it was not.

"Until one has loved an animal, a part of one's soul remains unawakened."
Anatole France

HOW DO I FIND MY REBORN PET?

I'm sorry, I don't know. Nor do I have a story on the subject. Nevertheless, I would like to say something about it.

My wife and I are enthusiastic sailors. Over ten years we had a sailboat at the Steinhuder Meer (German lake). At our jetty there was a married couple, in their late fifties, Helga and Heinz, who had been sailing for decades. We got along well. Our acquaintance was limited to more or less random meetings on the weekends while sailing.

When we brought our boat into the water for the start of the season a few years ago, Helga and Heinz were also there, but without a boat. Both were very sad, because Helga could not move her right arm anymore. Arm and fingers looked like they were inflated. So you can't do anything on a boat. The doctors could not help her so far. They didn't know what the cause was and therefore not what to do about it. The problems had come from one day to the next. Helga had been on sick leave for months and it was clear that she would lose her job in a small handicraft shop.

During our conversation I remembered my grandma. She was an extremely pragmatic woman and would have made cabbage rolls in such a case. Just wrap white cabbage around the arm with the help of a bandage, change it every few hours and that for a few days. When I said this Helga, she got really annoyed. She said: "Now you also start with this nonsense. My physiotherapist and my mother have already said that. We're not living in the Middle Ages."

I would like to write now that the cabbage wraps helped, but no, Helga did not try them. When I met her a few years later by chance in Hannover, she carried her arm in a sling. She was also very bloated, probably from cortisone. The doctors couldn't help her. They had sold the boat and Helga had lost her job. Maybe simple cabbage wraps could have prevented all this, but maybe not. We don't know.

There's a quote by Rumi:

Not only the thirsty seek the water - the water seeks the thirsty.

In this case the cabbage wraps came to Helga three times, I would have seen that as a sign, but already the first time. If you, dear reader, think it is possible that the soul of your pet will come back to you and you want it to, you have to keep your eyes, ears and heart open. Pay attention to signs and coincidences in this context.

If you say: "I would like my Putzi back and she has to be a little black cat again and should look exactly like Putzi", it will probably be difficult.

You read it in this book, the soul can come back, but sometimes in a different shape than before. So what, perhaps it is even better this way, who knows in advance.

There are no coincidences, everything is purpose.

Here's a joke to match:
A man is sitting alone in his house. It's been raining for days. The river rises over its banks, the water flows into the cellar, then floods the ground floor. The man goes into the attic. When he looks outside, all he sees is water everywhere. He starts praying, "Dear God, please save me." but the water keeps rising. He has to climb up on his roof.
The water's rising. There's a life ring floating by. The man is thinking about whether to use it, but decides to continue praying. "Dear God, please save me."
The water is still rising. In the meantime it has reached the chimney. The man climbs up the chimney. There's a big block of Styrofoam coming straight at him. He doesn't catch it, but continues to wait for God to intervene.

The water continues to rise. Meanwhile the man is standing on his chimney with his feet in the water. A huge old oak tree drifts by, so dense that he has to avoid its branches. He considers whether he should climb this tree, but decides against it. A short time later he is carried away by the floods and drowns. He goes to heaven to God and complains to him: "Why didn't you save me? I have always been a good person and have lived the way you want me to live. Why did I have to die?"

God looks at him and says, "I sent you a life ring, a Styrofoam block and a huge, super comfortable, unsinkable tree. Why didn't you accept my help?"

FROM THE BERLIN NEWSPAPER

The Berlin Newspaper of November 4th, 2006 published an article with the following headline:

"Soul migration, this pensioner claims her husband was reborn as a dog."

In the article Helga B. (59) says about her dog Teddy "This is my husband Heinz. When he died, his soul passed over into this dog. When I looked into his eyes for the first time, I saw my husband. Heinz looked at me."

Helga B. is convinced that her deceased husband is still at her side in the form of her dog. Teddy gives her security, loyalty and good advice. He warns her of bad people and has given her life a meaning again. She says if he could, he would carry me on his paws.

By the way, if you can't stand it with humans at times, you have the animals.
Friedrich Theodor von Vischer, philosopher, poet, aesthete

THE MYSTERIOUS RUSSIAN WOMEN IN CHRISTIANIA

When my friend Werner moved to his new life partner Annie in Copenhagen a few years ago, I was happy with him. However, I have to admit that I was also a little envious, because he moved to Christiania on Annie's houseboat.

Christiania is for me the most interesting place in Europe, an alternative, autonomous settlement in the heart of Copenhagen. The city is administered in a grassroots democratic way, independent of state authorities. It has its own currency and flag. The whole city is car-free, the atmosphere is calm and relaxed, the residents are tolerant and friendly. You can already see that I would love to live there too. I especially like the architecture and the alternative dwellings. Last year I even saw a Mongolian yurt there, which was built on a huge wooden floating pontoon.

But now on to Werner and Annie. One day they had a new neighbour. She had sailed from Russia to Christiania with her small, old cabin sailing boat and used a empty berth right next to my friend's houseboat. The woman was extremely mysterious. Somewhere in her late thirties, early forties, she was always smiling, but never spoke a word, probably mute. She didn't use sign language, she only communicated by nodding or shaking her head. If she wanted to show something, she didn't use her fingers, but only looked at the spot. It is said that she understood every language because she communicated with everyone. At some point there was a rumour that she was also deaf and could read minds. Nobody knows what is true about this.

My friend told me on the phone that the Russian woman could make his terrier sit or lie down just by moving her head. She was also able to summon swans, ducks or geese telepathically, and to make them come ashore either to the left or right of the houseboat. When asked whether she could communicate with all animals, she answered with a nod, so yes. I found this all very interesting.

My wife and I have, as already mentioned, an Akita Inu bitch, Kita, she is a trained sled dog. She understands the terms used in sled dog sport and follows them. She doesn't know commands like Sit or Down, because we didn't teach her. We wanted an intelligent dog with personality, character and will of its own. Kita decides itself whether and when it lies. I would never tell my dog to lie down when meeting another dog. For me it is a sign of submissiveness. If she thinks she wants to do this, okay, but not on my order. When dealing with daycare, Stop is the most important word. She always obeys this command and in the twelve years that I have her now, I have needed no more commands in daily life than Stop and Here.

When we went to Sweden for our summer holidays, we naturally visited Werner and Annie. What could be nicer than sitting on a houseboat in the middle of Copenhagen in summer? We also got to know the Russian woman. I asked her in German if she could give my dog the order to sit or lie down. She nodded. Then I said that Kita does not know these commands and is also very stubborn, which made her smile a bit more than usual.

During the conversation, Kita lay sleeping on the floor between us. The Russian woman looked at me, looked at the cabin door, then at the sleeping dog and again at the cabin door. Immediately Kita got up and went to the door. She sniffed, sat down and a short time later she lay down. At that moment I still believed in a coincidence, but then Kita got up again, sniffed again, sat down and lay down a second time. Then the Russian woman looked at me, looked at my hands, then at Kita and Kita got up, came to me and licked my hands. More is not possible.

This woman was able to control my intelligent, headstrong dog like a puppet. What is that? What's going on? What force is at work?

What connection do we have with our animals? How much do we influence them and how do they influence us? I can't get Kita to do anything telepathically. Conversely it seems to work. Sometimes, when I sit at my desk, I think I could actually play with Kita for a moment. When I get up and go to the patio door, she is already sitting in front of it and waiting. Since I think about it, I feel that I can sense her desire for attention.

The fact that humans communicate with their animals occurs frequently, with wild animals not so often. Interesting is the case of Francisco Duarte. The Brazilian newspapers reported for years about this little and probably mentally retarded boy. He was able to "talk" with almost all animals. According to his own statement he also understood their languages. Francisco could touch poisonous snakes and give them the order to curl up or crawl into a jar. He could command bees to sit on a certain flower or handkerchief. He could also send them all back to their hive. Frogs would run backwards and spiders would start to dance if he wanted them to. The parapsychologist Alvaro Fernandez even reports that fish in the lake came to Francisco when he put his hands in the water and called them.

Some of this can be read in German on the internet, keyword "Kommunikation mit Insekten". Those who know Portuguese and have some time to search will find newspaper articles. There are also Youtube videos, but they are all in Portuguese.

Well, insects, snakes, frogs and fish can be manipulated by a small mentally retarded boy through the power of thought, but can this also be done with big, wild animals? Yes, it can.

The Hungarian neurologist Ferenc Völgyesi (1895-1967), he was a student of the neurophysiological school of the Russian physiologist and psychologist Ivan Petrovich Pavlov, known by the "Pavlovian reflex" named after him, proved that it is possible to hypnotize animals.

He has written a book about it, which is available in German "Menschen- und Tierhypnose" by Franz Andreas Völgyesi. I have read parts of this book. Völgyesi speaks of two kinds of hypnosis. Firstly, he says that animals have hypnogenic zones. For this the animal has to be touched at a certain place. Völgyesi used this method to freeze crocodiles and snakes, for example. Secondly, he speaks of being influenced by thought power alone. He proved this in the Budapest Zoo by freezing lions and bears by the power of his thoughts alone. There are very impressive pictures, but the comments are in Hungarian and the pictures are hard to find.

The studies of Völgyesi have unfortunately been forgotten. The majority of today's veterinarians consider it impossible that hypnosis works in animals. Now that the ladies and gentlemen should perhaps take a look at the photos of Völgyesi and his experiments or, even better, read his book or even continue his work or use his knowledge. No animal would have to suffer in a slaughterhouse anymore if it was hypnotized. With a cow, it is only a single grip on the chin, as Völgyesi proved. No dog would have to suffer the ordeal of an anaesthetic just to be x-rayed. One small grip in the right place and the dog is completely will-less for the next five minutes. According to Völgyesi, anyone can learn these techniques. We know so much and yet we know nothing.

It might be very difficult to convince a dog owner that his pet is not communicating telepathically with him.
Maurice and Robert Burton, authors

BELISSA – THE ONE'S JOY, THE OTHER'S SUFFERING

I found this story in an esoteric magazine from the year 2011.

On my 30th birthday I fulfilled a childhood dream. I acquired a cute cuddly puppy, a little Münsterlander and called her Bellissa. She gave me a lot of pleasure, was healthy, problem-free, eager to learn and obedient. Only when Bellissa heard children she became restless. She ran to them, sniffed around excitedly and then came back disappointed. One had the impression that she was looking for someone. This affinity to children I could not control even with the help of the dog school, but otherwise Bellissa obeyed very well and I could let her run without a leash.

One day I went jogging with Bellissa after lunch and we passed our playground where some dogs were already romping around. Since I knew the dogs, I let Bellissa off the leash. Completely surprisingly she did not run onto the meadow, but directly into the forest. She did not react at all to my calling and so I ran after her. In the last years I have participated in three marathons and I am at least as fit as my dog.

Fortunately there were no leaves on the trees yet, so I could see Bellissa all the time. She walked

76

evenly and seemed to be chasing nothing, it was incomprehensible why she was running away.

After about nine miles I lost sight of my darling when I had to wait at a road. Totally excited I called my husband, who immediately left his job and came with his off-road motorcycle to look for Bellissa, but she remained disappeared.

In my distress I called the police. The very nice policeman gave me Tasso's emergency number. This is an association that, among other things, keeps a pet registry and helps in the search for missing pets. I did not know Tasso yet. I was given the phone-number of a search dog center and there I found out that a volunteer search dog handler lives very close to us. What luck and how great a mobile phone is!

At first I only reached the daughter of the search dog handler and briefly described what had happened. The recall took place a short time later. "When did your dog run away and where are you now?" That's all she wanted to know. I should wait there and already a quarter of an hour later Katrin was there with her search dog Alex.

A quick hello and off we went. "Please place your dog leash on the floor." The dog sniffed at it and sat next to it. "That's not enough," said Katrin, "Do you have something in your pocket that be-longs to your dog? A toy, a ball, anything?" Unfortunately I didn't have anything suitable. So we drove to our flat and I got Belissa's blanket from the basket. Then we drove to the place where Belissa had escaped and Alex picked up the trail. It was fascinating. He ran exactly the way Belissa had taken, passing the old oak tree on the left and then into the forest in front of the bench. Alex had the trail.

In order not to lose any more time, we got back into the car and started the search where I had last seen Belissa. Alex ran along the road and found Belissa's trail. We continued through the forest. Belissa seemed to run straight ahead like pulled by a magnet, right through the forest and we followed her.

In the meantime my husband was back home. On the mobile phone I told him in which direction Belissa was running. With the car he drove in the same direction. Belissa was running at about six miles an hour. In the meantime four hours had passed, so she could already be 25 miles away from home.

When it got too dark in the forest, my husband picked us up. At first we thought about going ten to twenty miles further south to look for the trail with Alex, but then we gave up the plan because it was too dark by now.

During the night it rained heavily. The next morning Alex had problems to follow the trail. On a paved bike path he lost it and didn't find it again. On the map we looked where Belissa might have run to, but there was nothing there, at least nothing she knew, no place we have ever been.

Over the next few days we distributed profiles in several places and asked for help. We also offered a reward, but apart from a few nutcases, no one came forward. Belissa had an identity number tattooed in her ear, which we gave to veterinarians, animal shelters and the police with the request to inform us, but nothing happened, Belissa remained missing.

Three months later, I heard of a woman in Bielefeld who makes contact with deceased people, finds lost items, and allegedly has found out the whereabouts of runaway pets several times. Full of hope I called her. After a long conversation I transferred 150 € to her, sent a photo of Belissa and waited impatiently for a message. It took a week until she told me: "Your Belissa is very well. She is happy and now lives with a family she has been with before and wants to stay with".

Nonsense, we were the first owners. Belissa came to us as a puppy and we had already talked to the breeder. Disappointed and angry at the same time I called her. Again it became a longer conversation, which ended with me transferring another 150 € to find out exactly where Belissa was. My husband had no understanding at all.

A few days later we received an email with the location: B... in Austria! So our Belissa should live about two hundred miles away, in a small town in Austria. Thanks to the internet we found that this place has only about sixty houses. The claim that our Belissa should be there amazed us. My husband said that the lady in Bielefeld must either be stupid or exceptionally good. If she had indicated a larger city as her whereabouts, our search would have ended, because how should you find a dog there? However in a town with sixty houses, that was certainly not a big problem.

At the weekend we drove to B in Austria. We had a photo of Belissa with us and showed it to a woman who was at the mailbox. "This is Zimmermanns' dog, up the road, last farm on the left."

My heart was pounding. My face was bright red when we went to the farm. We got out of the car and Belissa came running to us, waving happily. The welcome was so stormy that I was knocked over and bent my glasses. Our Belissa, finally we had found her and in such an unconventional way. I was overjoyed.

What followed, however, was very hard for me. A man in his working clothes came out of the house and asked us to leave the farm immediately. We explained that this was our dog. Belissa even still wore our collar, on the inside our phone number was engraved in the leather. We showed the photo and the pet passport. The man ignored all this completely and became more and more loud, we too. Belissa disappeared in the house with her tail pinched.

Shortly afterwards a woman appeared with a baby in her arms and asked her husband to come into the house and us to wait. My husband immediately wanted to call the police and demand the return of Belissa. Finally we were in the right and could prove it. I insisted on waiting and already we had an argument: "Belissa is our common dog, but only because I wanted her to. I chose Belissa, bought and raised her. She ran away from me and I found her again. Belissa is my dog, so we do what I want." My husband went into the car, insulted and angry.

In the meantime several children had come out of the house, they just stood there and looked at us. The woman came to me, this time without a child, but with a photo album. She apologized for the behaviour of her husband. My husband got out of the car and loudly demanded the return of our dog. Then I had to apologize for his behaviour.

Belissa had also come out of the house, went to one of the children and let herself be stroked. She still wore our collar. I called her, but she did not come but lay down on the floor anxiously, as she always did when she had done something wrong.

The woman asked me where we came from. When I told her that we live two hundred miles away in Germany, she asked me if I had an explanation why Belissa had run two hundred miles and now lives here on the farm. I did not know any reason, but she did. She claimed that our Belissa was the reincarnation of her dog Wendy.

Just four weeks ago I would have laughed out loud, but in recent weeks so many extraordinary things had happened that my view of the world had changed. When I asked the clairvoyant in Bielefeld to find our dog, I entered a world of which I knew nothing until then. Now I was standing in Austria in the village the clairvoyant had told me about and a woman unknown to me claimed that my dog had run away to be with the family again, where he had lived in his former life. The woman gave the date of death of her dog, it was about eight months before Belissa was born. When she wanted to show me photos, I turned away.

Amazement, sadness, skepticism, despair - I felt all of these at the same time. Thoughts and images were scurrying around in my head. Belissa was obviously happy, she had voluntarily run the long way and apparently wanted to stay. Finally I gave Belissa's pet passport to the woman, took her in my arms and wished her, her family and our dog all the best. Then we went on a two hundred mile long, rather taciturn journey home.

"What we have once enjoyed we can never lose; all that we have loved deeply, becomes a part of us."
Helen Keller

MANY WORLDS

In the course of my 58 years of life I have got to know many worlds. The world of children, young people, trainees, the self-employed, etc., just like almost everyone else. In addition, I have got to know other worlds through my numerous hobbies and interests. As a teenager these were the world of interrailers, the world of discos and the world of motorcyclists. In later years the worlds of sailors, divers, mountain bikers, globetrotters, motorhome travellers, sled dogs and ornithologists were added, to name only the most interesting ones.

As colourful and varied as all these very different worlds were, all together they are not half as interesting, not half as colourful, as the world of energetic healing methods and the transmigration of souls.

FRANZ BECKENBAUER

Yes, the soccer star. He is said to have once said that his ability to handle the ball so well is related to the fact that he was a dog in a previous life. A friend of mine told me about this statement.

I could not find it on the internet. So I do not know whether it was meant as a joke or whether it even existed, but I found something else.

In an interview with the magazine Bunte in 2005, Franz Beckenbauer said that he had been studying the wisdom of the Far East for years and that he likes the idea of existing as a woman and becoming pregnant extraordinarily well in his next rebirth.

LUNA THE WHALE

This short story does not really belong in this book, because it is about a whale and a whale is not really suitable as a pet. Although, Sid's grandmother had one as a pet, but that's just a movie (Ice Age).

If you are interested you can read the whole story in the book "News from an unknown universe" by Frank Schätzing, only in German.

In March 2006 Luna, an almost worldwide known orca, died. The Muchalaht Indians in British Columbia believed that Luna was the reincarnation of their chief Ambrose Maquinna. Before his death, this chief had announced that he would be reborn as an orca. In fact, after the death of the chief, a young whale appeared, who lived constantly near the Indian settlement and was worshipped by the Indians. He allowed himself to be stroked, showed no shyness and allegedly even had the same grin as the deceased chief.

It became a well-known tourist attraction.

A similar story happened once before on the Pacific coast of North America about thirty years ago.

ECKI THE SQUIRREL

The summer was hot and dry. It had not rained for weeks and so I decided to clean the empty rain barrel from the inside. You can imagine how scared I was when I discovered a half grown, totally exhausted squirrel inside. First I put a bowl of water in it and put some cracked walnuts into the barrel. Then I scurried down to the cellar to get the rabbit cage from Dixi, because one thing was clear as daylight, if I release the little animal in this condition it won't survive. It is much too weak and the neighbour's cat is attentive.

The cage is open at the top. I make a cover from my old sweater and a squirrel bed from a towel. Then I get the squirrel and put it inside. It had drunk water, but did not eat. A few hours later it runs around in the cage and starts nibbling the nuts. It will be all right, I'm sure. Two or three days and it will be strong enough for a life in nature.

Actually I didn't want to give the fluffy squirrel a name, because a name is something personal, connecting and already a relationship is building up and that's exactly what I don't want anymore, but I simply had to call this squirrel Ecki, a person from a German crime series. He looks like Ecki, has eyes like Ecki, the name fits like a glove.

The next morning the shock, Ecki is gone, but I'm too stupid. I didn't realize the squirrel could fit through the bars, but I made a nice cover. Well, the windows and doors are still closed, Ecki must still be in the flat and where do I find him? At Dixi's favourite place, he sits there and looks at me. Animation program squirrel hunt is announced. I go into the bedroom and get a sheet that I want to throw over Ecki, come back and Ecki is gone. I search and find him in the cage. All the nuts are eaten. He seems to be comfortable. I go for breakfast and who is sitting under the kitchen table in the exact same place where Dixi used to sit for breakfast? OK - I say - you know your way around here, you must have been watching me secretly. I have breakfast and put a small piece of crispbread on the floor. After several attempts Ecki gets it.

This is the first time in two years since Dixi died that I have an animal in the house again. I'm glad I'm on holiday. Next day, my new resident really drives me crazy. He races around the flat, climbs and jumps on every cupboard, gets tangled up in the curtains and seems to have a lot of fun. Well, I guess our time together will end tomorrow, back to nature with you.

Sounds logical and simple, but it didn't work. In the morning I opened the terrace door wide, hoping that Ecki would run outside, but he didn't do me that favour. So I put the cage with Ecki in it on the terrace, then I went in the flat, he followed. I went out to the cage, he followed and went in. Well, I've a lapsquirrel for a year now. Ecki feels comfortable with me. He runs out onto the terrace, comes back in and sleeps in his cage, which he can leave at will.

A few days ago my esoteric friend Hanna came to visit me. She is of the opinion that Ecki is the rebirth of Dixi. She says Dixi wanted to come back to me, but because I didn't want to have a rabbit anymore, didn't want an animal at all, he had to come up with something. And so he was born a squirrel and then, relying on my well-known helpfulness, jumped into my rain barrel. Has anyone ever heard such nonsense?

I got this story from a rodent forum. I contacted the writer and asked her if she thought it was possible that her friend was right and Ecki was indeed the reincarnation of Dixi. Here is her answer.

Yes, you may print my email in your book, but without my name.

I am a devout Christian. In my faith, there is no transmigration of souls. I believe that I will see all my loved ones in heaven, including animals, of course. We will be united in heaven, not on earth.

The fact that Ecki visits the same places as Dixi is certainly no coincidence, but is connected with the good overview on these places. Maybe it' s also earth rays or maybe it's just not earth rays. Some animals instinctively choose such places. We humans also prefer certain places. Look, there are places that have been inhabited by humans for thousands of years. And a hundred meters next to it there is a place that looks the same, but there has never been a settlement. Some historians dig and dig and find that the deeper they go the older and older legacies of our ancestors come. It's just the localities, nothing else. There's nothing mystical.

That Ecki was so quickly fixated on me is simply due to his young and inexperienced life. I rescued him, gave him food, so it is logical for him to stick with me, so that he will continue to be well. Maybe he sees me as a kind of surrogate mother. It's a self-preservation instinct, nothing more. It has nothing to do with the fact that he knows me from his previous life. Probably this is not the answer you need for your book, but it is my conviction. Do you also dare to publish my critical opinion in your book?

DEPENDING ON YOUR POINT OF VIEW

Two adventurers meet in an oasis. One tells that he almost died in the desert. The other wanted to know everything exactly and asked what had happened. So the man told:

I broke down with my bike in the middle of nowhere with an engine failure. I waited two days, but nothing happened. On the third day I started to pray to God. I said, "Dear God, I have never believed in you, but now I am asking you to help me. Save me, and I will live and act in your spirit for the rest of my life."

"Oh" said the other one, "So God saved you? Otherwise you wouldn't be here."

"Nonsense" said the man "A caravan happened to pass by, I was already unconscious. They gave me water and brought me here."

BROWN BLUE

A neighbour lent me the German book "I've known my son for ages" by Ramona Hartlieb. The book was published in 1980, has 321 pages and was written for the son and family of Mrs Hartlieb. It is a great life story, which reflects a lot of knowledge, spirituality and wisdom.

I summarize the first part of this book, which is interesting for you, dear readers, in such a way that the sense and thoughts behind it are preserved.

Mrs Hartlieb and her husband had decided not to have children. They did not want to take responsibility. Both were enthusiastic glider pilots and motorcyclists, which are not safe hobbies. Successful in their profession, the years went by. Mrs Hartlieb heard the biological clock ticking, the wild motorbike time was over and somewhere in secret the desire for a child was there after all, but a child means responsibility, one's own life is controlled by others and so both decided to continue living as before.

The neighbours of the Hartliebs were an old married couple with an also old dog, an Australian Shepherd. This dog had a blue eye on the left and a brown eye on the right, which is more common in this breed. The dog was especially well known to Mrs Hartlieb, because she always had some time for it since its puppy hood. Sometimes she went for a walk with her neighbour and the dog, a good working neighbourhood. So it was also natural that she took care of the dog when her neighbour suffered a stroke.

From then on the neighbour was in a wheelchair. Her husband could not take care of her, the house with its many stairs was not wheelchair accessible and so they decided to move into a nursing home. The dog was not very well because of his age. It suffered from incontinence, had problems with its hip and should be put down.

But Mrs Hartlieb did not want that, because in the meantime the dog had been with her in the house for several weeks and although it was a lot of work, she had taken it into her heart. The daily routine was changed a little bit and the dog wore a special dog diaper so that it did not soil the carpet. They spent a beautiful summer together, this time for the first time there was no flight, but a dog-friendly holiday at the North Sea. In autumn the dog died and Mrs Hartlieb noticed that this dog needed constant attention and love just like a child. She had also noticed that she and her husband enjoyed taking care of this animal.

So the desire for a child came back to the surface, but the first child at the age of 43? Mrs Hartlieb went to a doctor and had a consultation. The next year her son Felix was born, a perfectly healthy boy.

Mrs Hartlieb writes in her book that she is convinced that the dog came to her to show her that she would be a good mother. He didn't come into her life by chance, but purposefully came to the neighbours to be near her. He couldn't go to her himself, because she and her husband didn't want either dog or child.

Mrs Hartlieb is sure that the soul of this dog has often met her in past lives, not in the form of a dog but as a human.

For her it is certain that this soul, which she has known for ages, as she writes in the title of her book, now lives on in her son and this has nothing to do with the fact that her son has a blue eye on the left and a brown eye on the right, just like the dog before.

"*If there is a heaven, it's certain our animals are to be there. Their lives become so interwoven with our own, it would take more than an archangel to detangle them.*"
Pam Brown

FOXI, THE DOG FROM THE OTHER WORLD

My wife's friend works at a nursing home. In this home lives a 75-year-old former lecturer who can only see dimly due to an eye disease. Nevertheless the lady takes part in social life, she is active in the singing group and whenever something is organized she is there.

One day the woman asked a nurse who actually owned the dog that is always in her room in the morning. He would have the same fur as her late Foxi and she would like to spend more time with him, but whenever she came back from breakfast he was already gone.

The nurse explained that for hygienic reasons no dogs may be kept in this house and that visitor dogs are not allowed in. She also reported the incident to the management, because it was obvious that the woman had hallucinations. In such cases, the administration of tablets is controlled, as there may be undesirable side effects. However, since the woman did not take any tablets that could cause hallucinations, she was observed more closely, in fact she was overheard.

In the morning, after getting up, she talked to a dog as real like it was actually present. However, during the course of the day no longer and the woman made an absolutely clear impression. One of her carers has dogs herself and one day brought her a bowl of water so that the dog could drink.

The lady started to laugh and said that she now knows that it is only the ghost of her deceased dog Foxi who comes every morning to keep her company. Then she said that she communicates with her dog by telepathy. Foxi had seen how sad she was at his death and that is why he decided to stay close to her and take care of her, but he could only stop by for a short time because he was in heaven and lived there in perfect harmony with other people and animals.

Furthermore, the lady claimed that when her dog communicated with her, she could see a sunny, slightly hilly landscape, not in her head, not in her memory, but with her eyes. Although she sees almost nothing else, she claimed that when her dog's spirit is there, she can see things that are somewhere far away and yet so close.

The lady said that two worlds overlap. The world we live in is, from her point of view, grey with houses, cars, planes and noise. The other world, however, was beautiful, bright, friendly, populated with happy beings, but these beings are neither human nor animal. They are disembodied but nevertheless present. Every living being in our world would come to this other world at some point. Some would stay there, others would go back to our world by being reborn, and still others would watch over the living as disembodied beings. They could shuttle between the worlds, like her Foxi. Every living being has to spend a certain time in our world, those who kill himself stay in this world. He will not yet see the other world.

A dead dog told an old woman all this. She is convinced that when her time comes, she will be picked up by her parents and Foxi and accompanied to the far near world.

IN MY COUSIN'S VILLAGE

My cousin has been living in a small town in Bavaria for twenty years. When I told her about my book project by phone, she had something for me.

In her village, a 98-year-old woman lives alone in a house on the outskirts of the village. She has never been married, has no children and lives in extreme seclusion. Already at school she spoke of the fact that she would be 103 years old. The woman has the reputation of a witch or healer, depending on who is talking about her. She conjures warts, shingles and treats sick pets by talking to them.

For as long as one can remember, the woman has always possessed a pitch-black tomcat. This tomcat is said to have died five times already and each time returned as a kitten three months later. No one has ever noticed where the young tomcat came from. It was simply back three months later. It was not from the village, that was for sure. Of course the gossip factory is working overtime.

When my cousin moved to this village, her mother-in-law advised her to put her thumbs in her fist whenever she passes by the woman's house or sees the woman somewhere, as this protects her from the evil eye. Furthermore, if she ever talks to the woman or comes close to her, she should spit out afterwards unnoticed and definitely put her thumbs into her fist. In the meantime my cousin has settled in well. She has friends in this and neighbouring villages, some of whom have children, and they all follow these rules.

Why am I telling you this? I want to express that even today, in the information age, we are still afraid of the invisible. We believe that something is possible for which there is actually no room in our enlightened world. Is there something deep in our subconscious or our genes that whispers to us "Beware Danger"?

My cousin is now fifty years old, has lived in the village for twenty years and, even if she only drives past the house in the car or sees the woman somewhere, she puts her thumbs in her palms. Better safe than sorry.

Quote from the old woman just described:

"Sometimes I see colours in people or animals, colours that are not there. When I see the colours, I know things about these people or animals that I cannot know. The colours say almost everything about illness, pain or character. I recognize weaknesses and disorders.

Sometimes when I look at photos of people, the same thing happens. Also there I see colours that are not there. And even then I know almost everything."

CÉLINE DION

At around 6.30 p.m. on 29 July 2011, in Atilla Sereftug's music studio, the Eurovision Cup,, fell from the place where it had stood for years and broke. He won the cup for Céline Dion's winning song "Ne partez pas sans moi" at the 1988 Eurovision Song Contest.

Attila Sereftug was producer and composer, but the lyrics were written by Nella Martinetti. Mrs Martinetti was always rather sad that the cup was not with her, the lyricist.

Mrs Martinetti died on 29 July 2011 at 5.30 p.m. One hour later the cup crashed down. Attila Sereftug is convinced that the soul of the very headstrong Nella Martinetti was in the studio and that this was her way of saying goodbye.

THE DOG THAT BECAME A CAT

I read your book "Cancer in Dogs" for no particular reason. I like to read a lot about animals. You write that you believe in soul migration. I don't believe in it, I know it. Every animal is immortal and every animal is reborn. Perhaps you have the time to read my very long email.

I probably smoked as much as our former chancellor Helmut Schmidt. Unlike him, smoking did not agree with me. In the meantime I am missing my right lower leg and one lung. I am 53 years old, my heart has only seventy percent of its capacity, I spend my days in a wheelchair in a nursing home. All very unpleasant, but it's my own fault.

When I was still healthy I had a medium sized mongrel dog for twelve years. My wife had brought Dabo into our marriage. He was only two years old at the time and I liked him very much. Every day in the morning before work I went with him to the meadow behind our house and played ball with him until he made a dog doo. After work we went for a walk every day, which usually ended in the pub. I know it's not much, but I still loved Dabo. I could have done more for him, but somehow I didn't.

When our marriage was divorced, my wife kept the flat including furniture, as "value compensation" I got Dabo. A short time later, I suffered a posterior myocardial infarction. Since I had no family and no friends, I had to give Dabo to an animal shelter for care. At that time he was already fourteen years old, but healthy. When I was released from the hospital, I immediately went to the animal shelter. There I was told that Dabo died completely unexpectedly just a few days after he was admitted.

Now I was sitting alone in my flat. My heart was so weak that I could not even go outside. I would have loved to have a dog again, but how could I take care of it, how could I walk it? Dabo made me a dog fan, another pet never occurred to me.

One Sunday morning, it was sunny and windless, I was sitting on my balcony with a coffee and the obligatory cigarette when I heard a whimpering sound. It came from the garden. I looked over the balcony railing, but I couldn't see anything. So I took my crutches and hobbled into the garden. In the light well in front of a cellar window I saw a little kitten sitting. It must have fallen in there. It was wet and seemed to be completely weakened. I couldn't get it out and had to ask some boys playing football nearby for help. They took the kitten out, gave it to me and before I could say thank you, they were gone again.

That's how I got Rhonda. Five years have now passed. I have an animal again who loves me despite all my faults and handicaps. Rhonda has some habits and quirks that remind me very much of Dabo. At first I thought that I was imagining it or it was just wishful thinking. In the meantime I am completely convinced that Dabo is back, this time as a cat. If he had been reborn as a dog, I would not have been able to keep him, how could I? I couldn't even take him for a walk.

Animals are the smallest part of the divine creation, but we will see them again one day in the mystery of Christ.
Paul VI, Pope

SOMETHING REALLY STRANGE

In Werl Prison an inmate convicted of bank robbery held a trial to enforce a visitation permit for his cat Gisela.

The reason: He as a devout Buddhist knows that this cat is the reincarnation of his mother. So he demanded that his mother, who now lives in the form of a cat, be allowed to visit him.

The district court dismissed the suit. Probably the judge was not a Buddhist.

MRS MEIER AND HER GUIDE DOG

Mrs Meier is active in adult education. Since she was 38 years old, she has been suffering from epileptic seizures, which occur very irregularly. On average she has one seizure a week. On the recommendation of her doctor, Mrs Meier tried to get an assistance dog / epilepsy dog in 2010. However, the health insurance company refused to cover the costs because the disability was not bad enough, so she had to pay for the costs herself.

There are some institutions and societies with different training models that offer such dogs. For example, you can buy a puppy and train it together with a dog trainer. This training costs about two thousand Euro and takes about one year. Another possibility is to buy a partially trained one or two year old assistance dog and adapt it to your personal requirements with professional help. It is almost impossible to buy a fully trained epilepsy dog.

However, there is a married couple living in England (both are epileptics) who only train epilepsy dogs. These dogs are adapted to their new master or mistress in a fortnightly holiday. The dog remains the property of the couple, it is left with a leasing contract. Mrs Meier decided to lease such a dog at a price of 500 Euro per month.

The dog has the task of warning Mrs Meier of a seizure, which he succeeds one hundred percent. About thirty minutes before an epileptic seizure Georg gets nervous. He runs around Mrs Meier in a circle, jumps up on her and makes howling noises. Thereupon Mrs Meier has to take appropriate precautions. At work or at home she lies down on an air mattress with raised side walls in a separate room and waits for the seizure. This way there is no risk of injury for her.

Mrs Meier generally does not notice that she is having an epileptic seizure. For her it always comes as a complete surprise. Thanks to Georg she can pursue her profession and lead a normal life, except for a few restrictions. That Mrs Meier deeply loves this dog, to whom she owes so much, need not be mentioned.

In winter of 2014 the shock, Georg limped. In the veterinary clinic, bone cancer in the right shoulder joint was diagnosed, prognosis incurable, maximum life expectancy six months. Mrs Meier went online and found my book about cancer in dogs and contacted me after consultation with the dog owners in England. The first thing to do was to relieve Georg of the now severe pain and make sure that he could continue to do his job.

In recent years I have gained some experience with painkillers within my self-help group. One very blatant case was Doris. She had very severe tumor pain due to her pancreatic disease. The doctor prescribed her morphine drops, which she should take as needed, but then switched to morphine plasters after a very short time.

Morphine, like almost all drugs, act differently in humans. Doris became lethargic, listless and apathetic, but the worst thing was that she lost her appetite and therefore did not eat enough. Within a few days she developed severe circulatory problems. She was already underweight anyway, but neither the doctor nor the pharmacist could help. The doctor recommended artificial nutrition and the pharmacist wanted to use astronaut food and circulatory aids.

It must be said again that the problems were caused solely by the painkiller. Well, the underweight had existed for years and was constant, but now Doris lost weight because she had no appetite anymore. This was clearly caused by the morphine plasters.

On the internet we went looking for an effective painkiller and found a remedy that is used in such cases in the USA and supposedly helps well, Marinol. The remedy has no approval in Germany, moreover it consists partly of tetrahydrocannabinol (medical marijuana) and is therefore prohibited. Doris spoke to her doctor, pharmacist and oncologist and received the same answer everywhere. The remedy is not allowed to be sold in Germany, furthermore one does not know whether it helps or is even harmful etc. Marinol is also covered by the Narcotics act and then everything is much more complicated etc.

Doris only made one crucial mistake, she did not ask whether there was a comparable remedy in Germany and neither the doctor nor the pharmacist had the idea to research it, but more about that later.

Someone in our group then procured Marinol without a prescription at twice the retail price, illegally. Sometimes a seriously ill person has to expend a certain criminal energy. Marinol was fantastic. It was better for the pain than the morphine plaster. Appetite returned, circulation problems disappeared. Doris was in a good mood again and came to our meetings regularly again. She was now a drug user before the law, but what the hell. The end justifies the means.

Now we had in our self-help group a well effective remedy against pain, which unfortunately could only be obtained illegally and at a high price.

On the package insert were the ingredients and as the German Cancer Research Centre had often helped me, I called them and described the problem. My conversation partner searched briefly in the database and said that there is a drug with almost the same combination of active ingredients in Germany, but that it is not a finished product, but a remedy that has to be specially prepared by the pharmacy, its name is Dronabinol. The information provided by the German Cancer Research Centre is simply fantastic in the field of conventional medicine. My interviewer also told me straight away that there would probably be problems with the doctor who should prescribe the remedy.

The reason why there is little information about Dronabinol is almost grotesque. In Germany, it is not allowed to advertise a drug that is covered by the Narcotics act, which includes Dronabinol. Even the blanket distribution of information to patients is not allowed. However, the attending physician can request an information sheet from the manufacturer in order to prescribe the drug and the pharmacist who mixes the drug can also request an information sheet about the production.

I called our pharmacy and asked for Dronabinol. There one had to inquire first and called back after a few hours. Yes, it is possible to mix Dronabinol, but you would need a special narcotic prescription from a licensed doctor, preferably from the oncologist, and the health insurance company would most likely not pay for it.

The pharmacy advised to clarify this in advance. A special narcotic prescription is issued for drugs that fall under the Narcotics Act. It is a special prescription *with three copies and is only valid for one week, after which it expires. Doris then talked to her oncologist to get Dronabinol prescribed, but he said that she was doing really well after all and he saw no reason at all to use a cannabis product. Doris then put the Marinol on the table and said that she was doing so well because of this drug that she had been taking for some time. The oncologist seemed very surprised, talking about irresponsibility and laws that were made to protect patients and that it was a criminal offence to possess Marinol at all. He was not interested in the fact that it produced good results. He refused to prescribe Dronabinol.*

Doris went to the family doctor and he said that he could not prescribe Dronabinol because it is not approved for cancer patients, but only for spasticity diseases and outside the indication list he could not prescribe such a drug.

So there was a remedy, but neither the oncologist nor the family doctor wanted to or could prescribe it. I called the German Cancer Research Centre again and asked what to do. There I was informed that the regulations for these remedies had been changed a few weeks ago and that any doctor may prescribe Dronabinol, as it has shown very good results with many forms of pain. Doris got her prescription.

Since two members of my cancer support group were using Dronabinol, it was no problem to test the drug on Georg for a few days and hooray, he tolerated the dose of one drop twice a day. He was doing very well. Of course it was not possible to get the drug for a dog, but Doris was willing to hand over a 10 ml bottle.

Georg was now free of pain, but the cancer continued to grow. One paw would have been amputated, but that is not possible with a shoulder joint. Now we tried to stop the cancer. During my research for my book "Successfull treatment of cancer in dogs" I came across a remedy in 2012 that does not cure cancer, but stops it.

It was sold over the counter and all the users I had recommended it to so far were talking about very good results, no matter if human or dog.

From 1917 to about 1935, the American doctor Dr. William Frederic Koch had enormous success with cancer patients. He was successful, but probably a bit unconventional, in any case he was expelled from the medical association and thus fell into oblivion.

In the 70s the German physician Dr. Hans Nieper was interested in his work. Dr. Nieper was also very controversial and this although he was one of the best doctors of his time. Why the medical profession did not like him becomes clear when you read his book "Revolution in Medicine and Health".

Dr. Nieper died in 1998 without having finished his work. One of his former colleagues, a pharmacologist, took up his unfinished work again in 2005. This was done on behalf of her employer, a Dutch manufacturer of dietary supplements. She and her team developed a purely plant-based cancer drug, based on the work of Dr. Koch and Dr. Nieper. They internally called it SC = Stop Cancer.

The product fulfilled all expectations. In animal experiments, it succeeded in stopping various types of cancer, especially in dogs. So SC was unceremoniously offered as a dietary supplement for dogs suffering from cancer, without name, without approval, and without a list of ingredients. It was only sold by a single veterinarian in Amsterdam. In addition, the product was also sold to people with cancer seeking help.

Probably at the end of 2014, the company owner got scared because the remedy was clearly a drug, one of the ingredients is medical marijuana, and as such it needs approval.

He sold his company and his knowledge of SC to a Chinese pharmaceutical company. For a while the remedy was still sold as described by the vet and also a Chinese pharmacy, then it disappeared. On the internet there is no information about SC, because it was never sold under this name, it had no designation.

It is currently no longer available in Europe. I think this is a great pity, because I am convinced that this remedy is a blessing for all cancer patients, even *though it only stops tumour growth and does not cure it. The patient gains lifetime.*

When we needed the remedy for Georg in 2014, the procurement was not yet a problem. We could simply order it by telephone in the Netherlands and received it cash on delivery. The remedy worked.

In August 2015, almost two years after being diagnosed that Georg had only six months maximum left to live, he slipped while playing and broke his shoulder joint, which was severely damaged by bone cancer. Georg was taken to an animal hospital.

In the evening Mrs Meier received a call from the clinic saying that her dog was completely restless and could not be calmed down. A short time later Mrs Meier had an epileptic seizure. Georg had felt this over a distance of about thirty miles.

I think he would have felt it too if there were 10,000 miles between them. Georg and Mrs Meier had established a connection and it worked, incredible as it sounds, regardless of the distance, but not only the dog had felt something. Mrs Meier had also felt that something was wrong with Georg. When the clinic called, she was just on her way to the phone, to ask how her dog was doing.

Georg had been operated on. They tried to stabilize the broken shoulder with bone cement and wire. In order to avoid a new fracture, the right foreleg was also completely amputated. Mrs Meier told me that she had severe pain in her right arm on the day of the operation. She felt her dog's pain, even though she did not know that the leg would be amputated because the doctor had only decided to do so during the operation. Georg unfortunately did not recover. He had to be put down two weeks later.

And now comes the absolutely unbelievable. Mrs Meier is convinced that Georg, or rather his spirit, is still with her. He continues to warn her about her epileptic seizures. Mrs Meier says she feels it. There is a restlessness around her that she cannot describe. It's the same restlessness that Georg has always been spreading. When this happens, Mrs Meier makes her preparations as usual and waits for the seizure. In the meantime, six months have passed since Georg's death. During this time Mrs Meier has had more than twenty seizures and she has felt every one of them, really every one of them, in advance. No, not felt, as she points out, Georg warned her. She decided not to get another assistance dog. She has Georg to help her from the afterlife.

CRANE

That story doesn't really fit in this book. It was told to me by Mrs A and I express it in terms of content.

Although the events are basically very sad, it is at the same time incredibly positive and beautiful. I just have to publish the story.

Mrs A lives near the Diepholzer Moornie-derung, an area where tens of thousands of cranes take a break every year in spring and autumn on their way.

Our son loved birds almost from day one. Over his cot a mobile with birds hung, maybe that was the reason. Other children wanted dogs, cats or horses, Micha wanted birds. So for his third birthday we gave him two parakeets. When Micha was five years old, we bought him a good pair of binoculars, with which he went into the garden every day to watch birds. He was especially looking forward to the autumn, when the cranes are resting in the corn fields. We can see and hear them well in the fields around our house.

At the age of fifteen Micha knew everything about cranes. He loved these animals and could not get enough of them. In spring and autumn he went to a birdwatching tower almost every day with binoculars, spotting scope and camera and always came home only when the last crane was in bed. This is usually one hour after sunset.

One evening in November he was riding his bike home and had to cross a county road as usual. At this point there is a speed limit of forty miles an hour. In our area people often race. The landscape is flat and clear, the roads mostly straight. There are almost never any radar controls and mostly there are locals on the road who want to get somewhere quickly. It was windy that evening and so Micha couldn't hear the car coming out of the long curve with over 80 miles. He was dead immediately. We had some birds engraved on his tombstone.

Micha was no longer with us, but life went on. We still have the responsibility for two more children. Alone, we would probably have collapsed. Two years later our daughter moved to Munich to study. We visited her and met one of her fellow students who had lost her boyfriend. She told us that she had enlisted the help of a hypnosis therapist who had helped her a lot, but not with hypnosis, but with something better. What, she didn't want to say.

We received the address and telephone number of the therapist and since it was very close by, my husband and I took a walk in that direction in the

118

evening. When we stood in front of the block of flats, the door opened and a typical Bavarian woman came out. She asked us something, but we did not understand a word. Fortunately, she could also speak standard German. It was the therapist. We explained our concern to her and since we were leaving a few days later, she named Sunday after the mass as our appointment. Probably everybody in Munich knows when that is, we didn't know, but anyway, we met on Sunday morning. It became the most interesting Sunday of our life.

The therapist makes contact with the deceased. She looks at a photo of the person, immerses herself in another sphere and speaks to the soul of the person who is no longer alive.

We were able to ask control questions in advance, which she answered. It was incredible, she knew things that only Micha could know. Finally the therapist asked: "Where are you and how are you?" A short time later, she herself gave the answer: "I am fine, I am what I always wanted to be. I live as I always wanted to live and I'm free like a bird."

My husband and I were deeply touched and shaken at the same time and let our tears roll.

The following autumn, for the first time since we owned our house, a crane landed in our garden, a beautiful, large, healthy, strong, proud animal. Micha - I knew it was Micha. I opened the patio door, but it flew away. I don't think that this crane knew who I was and that it came to me knowingly. I think that deep inside it felt that it belonged here.

When my husband came home from work in the evening, I told him about the crane that had landed in the garden, but without expressing my suspicions. Without hesitation, he also said: "Maybe it was Micha".

Two days later it was back in the garden. The other cranes were over three hundred feet away in the cornfield, but this one was in our garden, where there was no food for it. With the camera I took so many pictures through the closed window until the memory card was full. Then I got the mobile phone and took pictures and filmed until it was no longer possible.

Even on the weekend, when my husband was at home, the crane rested in our garden and again stayed an hour before flying to the others. I had picked up several corncobs from a field and spread them across the meadow, but the crane did not pay any attention to them at all. It didn't come to eat. Perhaps it felt subconsciously connected with us and the garden. The crane only came in this one autumn. I took several thousand pictures of it. After that, no crane ever landed in our garden again.

Mrs A did not tell her children anything at first. It was scary for her herself and she was worried that she might be considered crazy. When the family came together at Christmas, she showed the pictures of the crane and carefully expressed the suspicion that this crane was the soul of Micha. To their great surprise, both children thought this was possible.

"Grief is like the ocean; it comes on waves ebbing and flowing. Sometimes the water is calm, and sometimes it is overwhelming. All we can do is learn to swim."
Vicki Harrison

POETRY SLAM

In autumn 2015 I went to a poetry slam in Hamburg. This is a lecture competition where short self-written texts are presented to an audience. A young woman recited the following story, but in rhymed form. I thought it was great, unfortunately the audience didn't.

During the break I talked with my seat neighbour about this lecture and told her that I am writing a book about the transmigration of souls of animals. She looked at me and said, "I've got something for you." What she told me you can read after the first story.

How many dogs are there that eat gooseberries and currants and how many pick them themselves from the bushes?

We had such a dog, Fixi. Sometimes, when there were no more gooseberries hanging outside, he would carefully try to get to the berries inside the bush without getting stung. He was very patient and extremely careful. After he died of old age, we got the mongrel dog Dago from the shelter, a dear older dog. He ate neither gooseberries nor currants, as it is normal for dogs.

Our garden is open to the street and one day a completely filthy, starved young dog sat on our terrace. It had neither a collar nor a tattoo. Its claws were totally worn out and its fur was totally matted. At the shelter they were looking for an implanted chip, but couldn't find one. We were told that this dog had probably been a stray dog for a whole year. The owner could not be found, so we kept it.

Rasputin, as we had named him because of his wild appearance, developed extremely well. Sometimes we had the feeling that Fixi had come back, just a feeling without any particular reason. Then the berry season started and what does Rasputin do, he eats the gooseberries and currants, straight from the bush.

And now I ask again:

How many dogs are there that eat gooseberries and currants, and how many do they pick themselves from the bushes? And what are the chances that we have twice a dog that does this?

Most unlikely I would say. So I think it is much more likely that Rasputin is the reincarnation of Fixi. Yes, I believe that.

The second story:

Two years after the death of my father and my professional move from Göttingen to Hamburg, my mum wanted to have a dog as a constant companion. She chose a Jack Russell Terrier, probably also because there was a hobby breeder nearby and she had often seen the dogs there. She liked one of the puppies immediately. She would have loved to take it with her, but the little one was not yet ready to be given away. So she had to wait a few weeks.

My mother went to visit the puppy a few times and was really looking forward to her new flat-mate. Two days before she was supposed to get the dog, my mother fell off the ladder while hanging the curtains. In addition to a concussion, she had a broken leg and a broken wrist. It was a drama. She could not take the dog because she was in the hospital. I was in Hamburg and so I could not fill in. The breeder suggested that he give the dog to another interested party and my mother agreed under tears. We had already paid the dog, his papers were ready, but if you can't, you can't. The breeder was very accommodating, he refunded the purchase price and put my mother on the list of interested parties for the next litter.

However my mother did not want another dog, I don't know why. This would have been her dog, another one, no thanks. One year later my mother came to visit me in Hamburg. In our weekly newspaper there was a report about an animal shelter with the photo of a young Jack Russell. The dog was given away by its owners because the family moved to the USA for professional reasons and could not take the dog with them.

I would take it, said mum and ten minutes later we drove to the animal shelter. Mama liked the dog immediately and we wanted to have it, but now there was a problem, my mother lives in Göttingen and the shelter only gives dogs away within its sphere of influence. So it says in the statute. They cannot and may not act differently. Mum started to weep, but the employee had an idea. She said that there was a possibility that the previous owner could get the dog out of the shelter and then give it to mum without the shelter's mediation. She then called the family, we explained the problem and arranged a meeting in the shelter in the afternoon, but this meeting never happened.

As soon as I put the phone down, the employee asked my mother "What is your name. Where do you live?" Then she put the pet passport on the table and up there as the first owner the name of my mother was written. It was the dog that my mother had chosen as a puppy over a year ago in Göttingen and which she could not take because of her accident. Since she was registered as the owner, my mother was now authorized to release the dog from the shelter. Another short talk with the current owners and we could take it with us.

This dog wanted to be with my mum and he made it. He is incredibly stubborn. What he wants, he gets, just like my dad. Mum believes that my father's soul is in this dog and indeed, he has some characteristics that my father also had.

CONNECTED

The following story was told to me by the owner of a pet food store.

One of his customers had a medium sized mongrel dog, about five years old. Shortly after the man retired, his heart became diseased, which required major high-risk surgery. The man made all the preparations for his stay in hospital. His dog came to his daughter's family, who lived in the neighbourhood.

The dog knew the family very well, because he was often accommodated there for a few days. Everything went well, the dog had settled in quickly as usual and enjoyed romping through the garden with the eight-year-old daughter. At night he was allowed to sleep under her bed. He did not seem to miss his master. He ate, drank and seemed happy and relaxed. His master was getting better and better, the operation had gone well.

One evening at exactly 10.00 p.m. the dog began to get restless. He whined, howled, barked and could not be calmed down. When the phone rang, the woman thought that now the neighbours wanted to complain about the noise, but it was the hospital. She was told to come because her father's condition had deteriorated dramatically due to a heart attack. She drove alone to the hospital, her husband stayed with the children and the dog, which had been howling and barking non-stop for an hour in the meantime.

The man called a veterinarian friend because he didn't know what to do anymore. Just before he arrived, the dog stopped howling and lay down flat on the floor. Only a few minutes later the woman called, her father had just died. The dog must have felt it.

Unfortunately the story does not have a nice ending. The dog refused totally, did not eat or drink anymore. He also did not react to the children any more. The called vet said that as far as he could tell, he was organically completely healthy. He didn't know what to do. For one week the dog remained lying down, then he was so weak and dehydrated that he had to be put down.

A similar story is told by the German Chancellor Wilhelm Cuno (1876-1933). He had a sheepdog named Aco, who was always close to him. Although Mr. Cuno was only 56 years old, he fell seriously ill. The behavior and the temperament of Aco changed suddenly. The playful, wild dog turned into a calm, deliberate animal. One morning, Mr. Cuno was doing well, according to the circumstances, Aco began to whimper and howl. It must have been unbearable, because they took him out of the house and locked him in a kennel. The dog did not stop. For hours he howled. In the evening, Mr. Cuno had a heart attack and died completely unexpectedly. At that very moment, Aco stopped howling. We don't know what happened to the dog. The story is written in a 1933 issue of the Journal for Metaphysical Research.

My mother died of cancer at home in her bed at Christmas 2002. Her Labrador Asko was in the living room sleeping. When mother was dead, I brought him to her bed, as I had always done the last weeks, so that he could say good night to her. Asko was always happy when he was allowed to go into the bedroom for a moment.

As well this time. He went in, looked at my mother once and started snooping around the room like he was looking for her. He looked at me questioningly. He did not pay any attention to his dead mistress. It was as if he did not see her. Also in the next days he walked constantly searching through the flat. He became very depressed, that only changed when we bought a second dog.

FROM A HORSE FORUM

I grew up on a farm in the Lüneburger Heide (a flat heath landscape in Germany). We had chickens, pigs, cows, sheep, goats, cats and a large orchard and vegetable garden. It was never boring. Like many girls I wanted a horse, it should be a pony and I wanted to ride in a carriage. I had read an adventurous girl's book about it. My father lovingly called me a princess and could hardly refuse me a wish, even if it was not easy for him financially.

When I was eleven years old, Sebastian came to us, a somewhat older pony from a zoo where he was used to driving a carriage. A used carriage was also organized. Sebastian and I became great friends and had a lot of fun together. I took very good care of him every day.

When I was fifteen, I loaded my tent, sleeping bag and whatever else I needed into the carriage and drove with my friend Rita and her sheepdog Clarence for eleven days through the Lüneburger Heide. We always asked farmers to stay overnight on the farm. Mostly they offered us a room, but we never used it. We wanted to sleep in the straw next to Sebastian and Clarence. Whenever we knew where we were staying overnight, we called home and told them where we were. I think our parents knew where we were staying before we did, because we were never really far away from home, actually we took a drive around the neighbourhood. Nevertheless it was a great adventure and I learned a lot on this trip.

Sebastian died when I was 21 years old. We had to put him to sleep. Later, I took over my parents' farm and successfully put it on room rental. Of course we still have animals, but only to pet for my and the holiday children. When my daughter Connie turned fifteen, she wanted an Icelandic pony. She knew how to ride and I know myself how beautiful and valuable an own pony is. It absolutely had to be an Icelandic pony because it is so easy to ride.

We found it by chance on a horse farm. Actually we wanted to go to the "Pferd und Jagd" (horse and hunting) fair in Hannover that day, but I took the wrong exit and was stuck in the middle of rush hour traffic. No chance to turn around and no navigation system so I turned the next street right, then again right and where did we arrive? In front of a horse farm! A small break would not be bad, so we looked around. A gelding magically attracted me, five years old, a very good physique and even for sale. I liked him and exceptionally also my daughter, otherwise we would never agree. You can get to a horse that quickly. There was a bit of negotiation about the price and delivery, as we don't own a horse trailer and soon we agreed.

We agreed that our new Icelandic pony Timmy will be brought at the weekend after next. So there was enough time to prepare everything. Connie was very proud and immediately plunged into work. The stable was cleaned and repainted and while we were at it, we renovated all five boxes we have. Connie had the idea to offer trail riders bed and box on the internet. A good idea, because many are out of season and our guest rooms are often empty.

We also got my old carriage from the barn. I washed away the dirt of the last twenty years and I started reminiscing. I dreamed of going on tour with Timmy and Connie. First I dreamed alone, then I told Connie about it and we made plans together. However Connie wanted to go to Denmark right away and not just for a fortnight, but for the whole school holidays. Well, let's see.

On Sunday an employee of the horse farm brought us our Timmy. He was extremely nervous, actually untypical for an Icelander. He looked here and there, became visibly calmer and ran straight towards the stable. Actually he was supposed to go to the pasture, but we let him have his way, he should look at everything. Then something strange happened, in the stable Timmy went straight into Sebastian's box. The guy from the horse farm asked if Timmy had been with us before, because he obviously knew his way around. But he had never been with us before and he was not supposed to go into this box, it was not prepared at all, no litter, no water. So we tried to get him into the designated box, no chance. Timmy did not want to go into the prepared box, not even if all other boxes were closed and only this one was open. He then stood in front of Sebastian's box and waited until we opened it.

What can you do? After all, it didn't matter. Only I had a lot to think about. The biggest surprise was when Timmy saw the carriage. He was so excited. I had asked the previous owner if Timmy was trained as a coach horse, but he wasn't.

We have had the carriage repaired with new tyres and lighting. We got the right harness with all the trimmings and Connie found an experienced coach driver on the internet who was willing to make Timmy fit to drive. In return we offered him and his family our big holiday flat for the holidays.

Reiner first came from Schwerin to look at Timmy and the flat. He had brought his own carriage right away, because it allowed to be driven with two horses. He left the carriage with us and three months later Reiner arrived with his family and his fjord horse Poldi for training.

If a horse is to be accustomed to a carriage, it is much easier if it walks alongside an experienced horse. Timmy and Poldi got along immediately. After two days acclimatisation Reiner dared the first attempt. Timmy had no problem being harnessed in front of the carriage next to Poldi. Reiner did the first lap on a cart track. When he came back he said: "Timmy has run in front of the carriage one hundred percent. He behaved perfectly."

A few days later we took our carriage, with Timmy alone and me next to Reiner. After an hour I took a seat on the coach box, I felt like I was fifteen years old. Timmy was walking safely and relaxed. Reiner then called the previous owner, but he couldn't explain why Timmy was walking in front of the carriage.

I have an explanation. You can laugh now, but I believe that the soul of Sebastian lives in Timmy.

"Such short little lives our pets have to spend with us, and they spend most of it waiting for us to come home each day."
John Grogan

THE VEGETARIAN DOG

During a bicycle tour I met a woman with her dog. We got to talking. I told her about my book project, whereupon she told me the story of her dog, which she wrote down at my request and here it is.

We live near Vechta. Many years ago my husband got a job as an electrician in a slaughterhouse after a long period of unemployment. In the evening of the first working day he sat in our kitchen, weeping, and told me about the slaughterhouse. Since that day we are vegetarians.

My husband always wanted to have a dog and when he retired, we bought a sheepdog puppy. This happened after long deliberations, because we did not want to have a carnivore in our house. We asked around, we do not like to use the internet. It is possible to feed a dog vegetarian. So we did that.

Rex grew up big and strong. My husband took him to the dog training facility every week. Rex was faster than all the others and he was much more resilient, as well as calm and balanced. We never told anyone that he didn't get meat or normal dog food. As a reward we gave corn rings as a treat. These are actually meant for horses, but Rex loved them, just like all the other dogs we know and gave them to. The other dogs at the dog training field often got sausages after the evening barbecue. Rex never touched such things. He sniffed it, nothing more. He really did not like meat and sausage. As vegetarians we always eat a fresh grain porridge in the morning and because Rex liked it too, I always prepared twice the amount, we the one half and Rex the other half. The fresh grain porridge consists of freshly ground grain, which was soaked overnight, and fresh fruit, nuts, honey and cream.

Rex died in our car in a rear-end collision when he was five years old. It was dramatic. My husband became depressed and had to spend a long time in a clinic in the Harz Mountains. A year later our former vet called us. She said that she had a beautiful young German shepherd dog mongrel which the owner wanted to give away because it was not eating properly and he didn't have the time to take care of it sufficiently.

We had a look at the dog, the owner said that it only eats rice with carrots. It was terribly thin. You could see all its ribs and even its spine. My husband said that he had a special dog food and when it eats it, he would be happy to take the dog. With this special food he meant our fresh grain porridge. The next day we went there again and lo and behold, the dog ate the bowl completely empty and then continued to lick at it. Of course we took it with us.

After only three weeks Flash had a reasonably normal weight and my husband went with him to the dog training field for the first time. What happened there was strange, Flash immediately ran to all the dogs that Rex also liked to play with. He knew immediately what he had to do. It was like he knew everything.

It's like Rex is back. Flash has the same likes and dislikes as Rex and he also always sleeps next to his basket. Plus, he doesn't eat meat or sausage.

In a dog forum a woman reports, while browsing the page "Mongrels looking for a home" she rediscovered her dog, which died three years ago. She put the photo of the puppy next to the picture of her deceased dog. Both dogs have exactly the same very striking coat colouring with an almost distinctive pattern. For various reasons the woman did not take this puppy to her home. So the similarity remains, nothing can be said about the character.

READ IT ON FACEBOOK

I really screwed up. I saw a funny video on You-tube where a cat is scared of a cucumber. Great I think, let's see and put a cocumber secretly behind my Minka as she eats. Minka turns around, sees the cucumber, runs off, crashes into the glass and is dead. She has turned eight.

It looked so funny, safe, a joke, nothing more. And then my little darling died and I even filmed it. I cried, and then in the flat in town. Where to put my dead baby. I wish I could have died too. Minka in the car, off to mummy in the garden.

I almost had an accident because of all the crying. I buried Minka and bought roses on her grave and an engraved stone "We will never forget you". Then I let my mum console me and called Dirk to explain why I am not at home.

Nonsense, he says, Minka is mewling here, she's somewhere in the flat, listen! And indeed, I can hear Minka on the phone. Her ghost, I think it's her ghost.

In the night again and again the mew. Three nights I haven't slept at all. I heard it, Dirk too and Mom didn't want to believe it. Has come in the evening and has also heard it. Minka is still in the flat as a ghost. Neither of us can stand it. We'll move in with Mom.

For all living things are divine!
William Blake, poet

THE SOUL WEIGHS 21 GRAM?

In its March 11, 1907 issue, the New York Times wrote in an article about the doctor Duncan Mac-Dougall that he had determined the weight of the human soul.

MacDougall was convinced the soul takes up space and everything taking up space must also have weight. He had a precision scales built that could determine the weight of a bed with a person in it to within five grams. With this scales a person should be weighed while dying to determine the weight of the soul.

MacDougall wrote about this in the journal American Medicine: "Patients with a disease leading to severe exhaustion, whose death is associated with as little muscle movement as possible, seemed to me to be most suitable because the scales can be kept in perfect balance and any weight loss is immediately noticed".

People who died of pneumonia, for example, were not suitable. They would "fight enough to throw the scales off balance". Tuberculosis patients whose last moments were extremely inactive proved to be the best test subjects.

Six dying people weighed MacDougall, but only one measurement was actually meaningful. It was the aforementioned 21 grams. One of the main reasons why the other five measurements were useless was that the dying process in these people took too long and could not be properly recorded. The scales showed a weight loss of a few grams at the moment of death and then again the weight as before death.

On March 12, 1907, the Washington Post quoted Dr. Carrington's suggestion from New York "How much more satisfying it would be to have test subjects who were normal, perfectly healthy men". He seriously suggested hanging an electric chair on a scales and determining the weight before and after the execution. At that time, one could already be sentenced to death if one had stolen goods worth more than ten dollars and had the wrong skin colour. Serious thought was given to this, but failed due to some technical problems.

Because the experiment with humans produced such different results, MacDougall decided to repeat the experiment with dogs. To do this, a large weighing pan was hung on the precision scales, a dog was anaesthetized, placed in the weighing pan and then killed with a lethal injection. A total of fifteen dogs weighing between fifteen and forty pounds were "examined". None of the dogs showed a permanent weight loss at the moment of death, but all of them initially wavered by a few grams and then returned to their original weight.

In principle, this was the same result as before with humans. Dr. MacDougall could not explain this. One of his closest colleagues, a Frenchman, of whom only the initials Dr. F. D. are known, had an explanation why the weight of humans and also of dogs at the time of death first falls and then rises again.

He said: "The soul escapes at the moment of death. So the weight falls, then the soul sees the dead body lying down and immediately goes back in and so the weight rises again. He said that the soul needed some time to say its final good-bye, that one had to observe the corpse longer, because the soul would go out a second time. Mac-Dougall considered this thesis to be "mischief in the extreme".

The opinions of the experts on the weighing of souls diverged widely. Anyway, the soul weight of 21 grams has been haunting literature for more than 100 years and, of course, recently the internet. In 2003 the film "21 GRAMS" by Alejandro Gonzalez Inarritu was released in the cinema. As the name suggests, this film is about the weight of the soul.

But the story doesn't end here, on the contrary, now it just starts to get interesting. In 1909, the

French doctor Dr. F. D. went back to his hometown Marseille in Southern France. Here he carried out an incredible experiment with two scientific assistants of his clinic.

Dr. F. D. was of the opinion that the soul has a life of its own. He believed that it is possible to kill a dog in a way that the soul does not notice. In the spacious basement of his clinic he set up a precision scales and trained a dog to sit on it. When it did so, it was rewarded with a small cookie from a staff member sitting next to the scales. In another cellar room far away, Dr. F. D.'s second employee sat and gave a cookie to the dog every time it came to him. The dog constantly ran back and forth between the two employees. It did not get anything else to eat and so the dog was on the move for hours. Its weight was not recorded because it was not important for the experiment at that time.

In the evening, the dog had just picked up a cookie and was on its way to the scales, Dr. F. D. shot the poor animal. A few seconds later, the scales tipped out exactly 21 grams. The dog was dead. It was lying in the hallway, ten meters from the scales, and the scales showed 21 grams, exactly the weight of a soul.

Dr. F. D. cheered: "The soul went to the scales alone". To be on the safe side, Dr. F. D. and his colleagues repeated the experiment with another dog a few days later. The result was the same.

Now the three scientists wondered where the dog's soul would go and made a third attempt. The procedure was the same as described above, but after Dr. F. D. had shot the dog, which in the meantime had been running back and forth for several hours, he took it as fast as lightning and threw it into another room. Both employees stayed in their seats and continued to hold a cookie for the dog and then the incredible happened. Every few seconds the scales showed the weight of 21 grams. So the dog's soul continued to "run" back and forth between the two employees at the same speed as the dog had been running before. The soul had not noticed that the dog's body was dead.

Dr. F. D. triumphed. His experiment proved he was right. Now he could explain why the MacDougall's measurements showed these fluctuations.

Now Dr. F. D. had an extremely stupid idea. He wanted to repeat the experiment in the presence of some high church representatives and contacted the bishop of his region. It was the year 1909, the Church had a very strong influence at that time and of course they would have been interested in proving that man has a soul that can be measured by weight, but the Church had no interest in proving that a dog also has a soul. Human is the crowning glory of creation. He was created in the image of God, his soul goes to heaven after death. A soul in an animal and then still with the same weight as in a human - unthinkable.

Dr. F. D. and his team were supposedly granted an audience with the Pope, but never returned from this trip. With them disappeared all documents such as measurement results and evidence photos.

My opinion:

My book is about the soul, so I think this story is a must. I took the first part from the book "Das große Buch der verrückten Experimente" ("The Big Book of Crazy Experiments") by Reto U. Schneider, a much-praised book which was even Science Book of the Year a few years ago.

The second part, more precisely everything about Dr. F. D., I have from an English page entertained by conspiracy theorists. Among the members are also doctors and scientists. So the whole thing is no fake, the experiments really existed.

To the actual experiment of the MacDougall:

There are photos on the internet that show the "bed weighing machine". In my opinion this is absolute crap even for the conditions at that time. With such bumbling rubbish there can be no meaningful measurements. The friction losses are much too high, and in addition, completely unsuitable materials were used in relevant places. Perhaps a talented metalworker should have been hired to build the weighing equipment.

Everything about Dr. F. D. I think is not true. I have no doubt that he conducted those experiments on the dogs, but I doubt that he had any results at all. However, I think it is quite possible he was believed at the time. On the above-mentioned side of conspiracy theorists, the focus is mainly on the atrocities of the church and what is probably all stored in the secret archives of the Vatican.

I am convinced that the soul has no weight. If it had weight, we would know it. Today, with our technical knowledge and skills, it is no problem at all to weigh a dying person at the moment of death, accurate to the thousandth of a gram. All you need is a liquid-filled mattress, a sensor and a measuring device. 250, maybe 350 £, some knowledge and skill, three days of work and you have a perfect weighing device. The claim that the soul weighs 21 grams has been circulating in the press for decades. Then a few years ago there was the film mentioned above.

I maintain at least one thousand people have come up with the idea of weighing a dying person. There are so many creative people in the world, it can't be otherwise. Assuming someone would prove the soul actually has a weight, that person would be famous in one fell swoop He would give interviews, be invited on talk shows and so on. In addition to fame, if he did it skilfully, he could get rich from his interviews. Believe me, many people have had this dream.

So we can assume the experiments of both MacDougall and Dr. F. D. have been repeated many times. Since no one has yet come up with any proof, they do not exist.

THE MOUSEFREE HORSE FARM

In the south of England, Arthur Grower's daughter runs a horse farm. There are mice on every horse farm, but not on this one. "You can put a cheese in the corner for a week and nothing will happen to it" says Arthur. The reason is Zio, a ghost cat.

Zio was an extremely quarrelsome tomcat during his lifetime, he tolerated neither dogs nor cats on his farm and he was a good mice hunter. Unfortunately he got under the hooves of a horse and died. Up to that time there had been plenty of mice, despite Zio. However, after Zio's death they suddenly became fewer and fewer until a few days later they disappeared completely and never appeared again. Arthur Grower explains it like this:

When a spaceship races through the infinite universe at infinite speed, it is at all points in space at the same time. This has been calculated by astrophysicists and mathematicians. It's the same with Zio. As a living cat, he had only one speed, that of a cat. If he was in front, he couldn't be in the back of the stable. So the mice had a chance to avoid him. Now that he is dead, he is as quick as a thought, that is, he can be anywhere at the same time, and so he became unpredictable for the mice, and so they preferred to disappear.

The one who does not believe in immortality is like someone who denies the sunrise because he is blind.
Carl Ludwig Schleich, doctor, writer

THE SHAMAN

Mrs Breuer, a former dentist, lives in Bremen with her dog Othello, a Border Collie. She bought the dog after the death of her husband. Unfortunately Othello had problems driving. Not that he didn't want to, on the contrary, but he got sick and after a few hundred meters he started to gag. Once he already vomited when the engine was started.

Mrs Breuer sought advice from a veterinarian, but the given sedatives did not help. So she continued to search for a solution and found a shaman near Nienburg who produces highly energetic globules, especially designed for the dog's problems.

For this the shaman needs a detailed description of the problems, a photo and some hairs of the dog. The globules were effective and from then on Othello drove in the car without any problems. The nausea belonged to the past.

Unfortunately Othello was poisoned at the age of eight. Mrs Breuer had a nervous breakdown because she had witnessed the agonizing death of her beloved without being able to help him. For several weeks she hardly ever left the house and had to cry constantly. Her family doctor prescribed her antidepressants. Since Mrs Breuer herself has a medical education, she knows about the problems of such drugs and was looking for an alternative. Then she remembered the shaman. She called her and asked if she could get specially produced globules against depression. The shaman said that she only makes the globules for dogs and would not make an exception, but she had another idea.

The shaman suggested to bring back the soul of the dog from the afterlife, but not in the form of a newly born dog. She wanted to bring back the disembodied soul of the deceased Othello. Mrs Breuer agreed. The shaman instructed Mrs Breuer to obtain as many paper photos of Othello as possible. Furthermore she had to get a tuft of dog hairs from Othello, which were still abundant in the flat. In addition, Mrs Breuer was also to buy a large toy dog, which looks similar to the deceased Othello. That was quite easy, because Othello was a Border Collie and this type of dog is well available as a soft toy. She then used a felt-tip pen to paint the black spot over the left eye on the soft toy dog, which was so concise for Othello.

When Mrs Breuer had everything, the shaman came to her house. She said that the soul of Othello was still here on earth and did not know where to go, so it had to be offered a new body. This body should be the soft toy. The shaman started by distributing the photos of Othello all over the flat on the floor. Then she put the soft toy dog into the dog basket and attached Othello's hair to a paw with an elastic band. She filled the water bowl with water and the food bowl with dry food. Then she opened the patio door, lay down on the floor next to the dog basket and went into deep meditation. During this meditation phase, which lasted about one hour, she contacted the soul of Othello and told it to come home.

Mrs Breuer sat in the living room during the whole time and watched incredulously. While the shaman was still lying on the floor and meditating, Mrs Breuer felt that something was changing. Then she felt a wet nose on her hand and knew that Othello was back.

When the shaman told me this story, I asked if it would be possible to talk to Mrs Breuer. It was possible and since I am often near Bremen, I visited her once. During my visit Mrs Breuer told me the following:

Othello's soul is back. It's here, I can feel it abundantly clear. He walks through the flat and in the morning he stands at the terrace door and I let him into the garden. I change his drinking water every day although I know he can neither drink nor eat. Nevertheless I change it so everything is as he knows it. I also go for a walk with him, but without a leash, but I feel he is with me. Most of the time I walk his favourite paths and when there is nobody to see I talk to him. I have a dog again.

Othello always liked to ride in the car and when I drive away now, I go into the garage and open the tailgate so he can jump in. Actually it has always been my dream to buy a small sports car, but I won't because Othello needs the tailgate to get in.

I am seventy years old now, at that age I don't want to buy a new dog. I am single without a family. What would happen to the dog when I'm no longer here? That's better. And one day, when I die, I'll know who's waiting for me in the next world.

This story is hard to believe even with a lot of good will. If I had read it on the internet or elsewhere, I would not believe it. Maybe it is all based on Mrs Breuer's wish to be reunited with her dog.

I know the shaman since 2010. She is specialised in dogs and has helped many dogs I know with her globules. Here are just two examples.

In Bad Eilsen, our neighbouring village, lives a small mongrel dog named Nucki. He had a panic fear of leaving the house in the light, which caused his owners almost insoluble problems, especially in summer. I met Nucki and his mistress a few years ago, when I went for a nightly walk through the just fallen snow in winter together with my wife and our dog. She told me about her dog's phobia and I gave her the shaman's address. Months later she thanked me on the phone, the dog had lost his daylight phobia.

The shepherd dog of a former work colleague had been suffering from cystitis again and again for years. He got the globules for a few months and has never had a cystitis again since then.

These are for me proofs of the shaman's skills. In the first case it is a state of anxiety, thus a mental disorder. In the second case it is a cystitis, thus a physical disturbance. In both cases, which are very different, the shaman could help. Nevertheless I find it hard to believe that she can bring back the soul of a deceased dog from the afterworld.

"When we adopt a dog or any pet, we know it is going to end with us having to say goodbye, but we still do it. And we do it for a very good reason: They bring so much joy and optimism and happiness. They attack every moment of every day with that attitude."

Bruce Cameron

THE MAGPIE

In Sweden near Mora lives a man named Gunnar. When Gunnar was eleven years old, he found a magpie that had fallen out of its nest and raised it by hand. The magpie developed splendidly and always stayed near the house and sat next to Gunnar when he was doing his schoolwork outside. Gunnar named her Marina after the song by Rocco Granata. Marina died at the age of about ten years. Gunnar found her dead under a birch tree. Sadly, he buried his longtime companion.

The following late summer, a very young magpie sat in the garden, right where Marina was buried. At first Gunnar didn't worry about it, but the magpie came back every day. When Marina was still alive, Gunnar used to call her by whistling the song Marina. One day he whistled the song and the strange magpie flew to him and sat down on the ground a few feet away from him. Gunnar approached the bird and spoke to it. Then he walked towards the house and the magpie hopped behind him to the front door, just like Marina had always done.

Marina was back. Gunnar was firmly convinced of that. Their happiness together did not last long. Marina was killed by a fox in the garden the same year, but at the end of the next summer there was a young magpie in the garden again and she too reacted to the theme song.

Gunnar is now 64 years old and there is still a magpie close to him all the time. "It is now the eighth rebirth," says Gunnar.

Furthermore he says that he is not a believer and that he has never dealt with rebirth or anything similar. "In principle, I don't care about any of that. I do not even know how many grandchildren our king has, simply because I do not care, but I do know two things for sure. One is that I live in the most beautiful country in the world and the other is that I will be reborn as a bear, because as a bear I am allowed to live here in this beautiful area. I enjoy protection and above all I do not have to work. For sure, I will come back as a bear. I tell Marina that almost every day, so she knows and waits for me. Then we will roam the woods together, she on my shoulder. We'll see how long we can enjoy it. Maybe two hundred years or more, we'll see."

"Animals have come to mean so much in our lives. We live in a fragmented and disconnected culture. Politics are ugly, religion is struggling, technology is stressful, and the economy is unfortunate. What's one thing that we have in our lives that we can depend on? A dog or a cat loving us unconditionally, every day, very faithfully."
Jon Katz

THE ANIMAL COMMUNICATOR

A family with three children from Euskirchen had fetched an approximately five-year-old mixed-breed dog from the shelter. A calm, well-balanced and well-behaved animal, which was given away by its previous owner without giving any reasons. The dog settled in quickly and everything was fine as long as all family members were in the house during the night. If someone was missing in the night, the dog did not sleep. It ran around the house the whole time, squeaking and panting, which was very annoying. The family tolerated this for a few weeks and although they had taken the dog into their hearts in the meantime, it was clear that it could not go on like this.

They contacted the shelter, but the previous owner had not reported any problems. Maybe she lived alone with the dog. A veterinarian gave the tip to get advice from a well-known animal communicator from Hamburg.

The animal communicator needed a photo of the dog, then she connected with its soul and had a conversation with it. She found out, that the dog had lived in the USA in its previous life and that its owner had died in a car accident on his way to the night shift. Since the man had lived alone and nobody knew that he owned a dog, nobody went to his house for several days. When the house had to be cleared, the dog was found completely exhausted and dehydrated, and had to be put down by a vet.

The animal communicator said the dog was afraid of being locked up at night, but probably only if the family was not complete. She suggested that at night, when not all family members are in the house, the balcony door should be left ajar so the dog feels like it can leave the house. And indeed, the dog saw the open door and slept the whole night in front of it. It was no longer restless.

Meanwhile the dog is satisfied when the door is leaning because it knows it can open it.

What's there to say? I can't give you any explanation. I don't understand how the animal communicator found out. To claim something that no one can verify is easy, but to solve such a problem at the first attempt and over a distance of several hundred miles shows either tremendous skill or immense luck. What are the chances that a restless, almost panicky dog can be calmed down by leaving the balcony door open a crack in the night? Extremely small I would say. Anyway, the problem is solved. The dog was saved from the shelter and the family from a bad conscience.

If there were no dogs, I wouldn't want to live.
Arthur Schopenhauer, philosopher

FROM THE TYROLEAN DAILY NEWS-PAPER

An interesting article appeared in the Tyrolean daily newspaper in July 2005.

Swiss woman, who also lives in Switzerland, had two dogs. When one of them died, the woman got herself a second dog again. Two years later the woman had a waking dream. She saw a black and white tousled mixed-breed dog and after this dream she knew that the dog could be found at the animal shelter Mentlberg, Innsbruck.

She called the animal shelter and asked if there was a young mongrel there that matched her description. And indeed, the shelter had exactly the described dog. The woman explained on the phone that she believed that this dog was the reincarnation of her Ombre, who died two years ago. The Swiss woman drove to Innsbruck and the animal keeper was speechless, with what joy the young dog greeted her. It was like its mistress had returned. The lady took the dog, now called Ona, home with her and her other dog greeted it like an old friend.

When commenting on this report in an Austrian forum, a user writes that he is convinced his deceased cat Tiffany sent him his present cat Maya.

Another user writes that he had a similar experience with his deceased mother and since then he thinks differently about people who report such experiences.

Every living being carries a light within itself.
Paul Claudel, writer

PLATO, ATLANTIS, ALIENS, THE REBIRTH AND ME

Between 348 and 347 B.C. Plato wrote down the history of the island continent Atlantis, which was lost 9000 years ago, in the Critias and Timaios Dialogue. He refers to a story that the Athenian poet and statesman Solon, considered one of the seven wise men, had heard in Egypt.

The amount of information Plato left us about Atlantis fits on fifteen book pages. In 1997, Bernhard Mackowiak found out during his research for his Atlantis book that the follow-up literature on Atlantis now comprised 20,000 volumes worldwide, which was four million pages with an average of 200 pages per book. According to an Atlantis researcher, this number has even doubled in the meantime and so Plato's fifteen pages became about eight million. Since about 2500 years the myth Atlantis lives in the minds of mankind.

Expeditions were equipped to find Atlantis. Every year, someone claims to have the latest knowledge about Atlantis and its location. By now, the names of the kings of Atlantis are known. It has been calculated that the plain where the capital was located had a length of 335 miles and a width of 225 miles. The Austrian scientist Otto Meck determined the area of the main island. He came up with about 77,000 square miles. There are drawings of Atlantis with fairly accurate dimensions. The capital Basileia, also called Poseidonia, has been mapped in all details. We know which temple stood where and that the huge Temple of Poseidon was built by Atlas the first High King. We know a lot about the energy supply and also that there were temples that were completely covered with silver. We know how the citizens lived and we know that Atlantis went down "within one bad day and one bad night". So we know almost everything about Atlantis. What we don't know is whether Atlantis ever existed, because there is no proof of its existence.

For more than 2000 years people have been searching for Atlantis, nothing has been found. Nevertheless, history remains in our consciousness without a single shred of evidence.

Do you know what an alien looks like? Although you've probably never seen one, you have a fairly concrete idea of its appearance. We owe this idea of aliens to the people who claim to have met aliens. Their explanations, whether true or false, are firmly anchored in our consciousness and subconscious. In countless films aliens appear and more or less they look like we imagine them. So as far as aliens are concerned, we have a certain expectation.

Let's get to dying. Here, too, people from our cultural circle have expectations. Almost every person with near-death experience reports the same. A bright light, music, a fast flight vertically upwards and you are in the afterlife, where deceased relatives are already waiting. Is it like that? I do not know. Could it be that everyone has the same near-death experience because they expect it? I don't think everybody lies about having a near-death experience. I believe that what they say or write is what they actually felt, but I don't know if it is true, because there is no proof here either.

The situation is quite different with rebirth or transmigration of souls. There is evidence of this, not one, not a hundred, but thousands, I will mention only three:

A fifteen-year-old South American illiterate speaks a language that has been extinct for centuries, a language only a few scientists understand. The boy is even able to explain the peculiarities of this language, not to just anyone, but to linguists. Where did he get this knowledge from if not from a previous life?

A seven-year-old child claims to have lived in another village sixty years ago. It draws an exact plan of the village and also knows the name. It can also give the names of the people who lived in that village sixty years ago and a check has shown that all the details were correct.

An eleven-year-old leads the police to a place near a bridge and claims that he was murdered in his former life and buried there. The police investigate and find a case fifteen years ago in which a twenty-year-old woman disappeared without a trace. They dig at the site indicated and find her body. Not only that, the boy tells them who the murderer was and he confesses to the crime.

Are these supposed to be coincidences, spins, reveries? Certainly not. At the beginning of this book you read the story of my dogs, in which I confess that I believe in soul migration and rebirth.

Yes, I used to believe in it, now I know that it's true. I don't have to believe anymore because I know it. Soul migration and rebirth are not reserved for us humans. It applies to all living beings. There's transmigration of souls. This is my absolute conviction, the evidence is there, anyone can find it.

Sometimes losing a pet is more painful than losing a human because in the case of the pet, you were not pretending to love it."
Amy Sedaris

A REQUEST

Dear reader!

If you like my book, please help me and other readers by giving an honest review. Please recommend it to your friends or on Facebook and other online portals and help to make the book known.

I am convinced that after reading this book, many people will see their pet and all other animals from completely different perspective.

Just like humans, every animal has the right to live in freedom and peace. Let us together create a better world for humans and animals.

Norbert Kilian

(Vegetarian since 2006)